D1097363

HOW . . . much longer will Willie Mays play after he hits his 600th home run?

CAN . . . Denny McLain repeat his amazing 31-game year of 1968?

WHO . . . wins general acclaim today as baseball's "most exciting player"?

WHAT . . . National League team has the best chance of cutting down the Cards this year?

IF . . . you had one game to win, who would you pitch: Gibson, Marichal, McLain, Lolich or Tiant?

The answers to these and hundreds of other up-to-the-second diamond puzzlers are all in this sparkling edition of BASEBALL STARS OF 1969. In these exciting and dramatic pages, chock full of the stories told by America's top sportswriters, you can relive all of the unforgettable moments of the 1968 season and get the inside story on what to expect in 1969.

BASEBALL
STARS OF 1969

edited by RAY ROBINSON

PYRAMID BOOKS NEW YORK

BASEBALL STARS OF 1969

A PYRAMID BOOK

First printing March, 1969

Copyright © 1969 by Ray Robinson

Cover Photograph by UPI

All Rights Reserved

Printed in the United States of America

PYRAMID BOOKS are published by Pyramid Publications, Inc.
444 Madison Avenue, New York, New York 10022, U.S.A.

CONTENTS

PREFACE

I am getting bored reading that baseball is the great national bore. I am getting battle fatigue reading that baseball is dying, that it is too dull, that its batting averages are too small and its strike zone too large, that its owners are too predatory, its leadership too vapid, its ball parks too big, its athletes too inept, its gloves too Gargantuan, its strategy, tactics and choreography too non-violent.

I am getting bored reading that baseball is "sick"—not because the sport is without its troubles and problems—but because it's a game that is still, in the eyes of many, beautiful, lovely, dramatic and exciting.

If it is "decaying," as announcer Howard Cosell keeps telling us, and if it will "gradually disappear," as that celebrated baseball thinker, Bill Veeck, has said, then something quite decent, pleasant, charming and civilized will have deserted our lives.

Many of us, you see, are still strongly opposed to abolishing the languid and aromatic summer day at the ball park. We still thrill to the split-second precision of the double play and the hit-and-run; the thwack of a swishing bat colliding with the center of a baseball; the wholesome community spirit aroused in cities like Boston, Detroit and St. Louis; the heart-pounding tension and agony of a bases-loaded situation—and all of those other precise rhythms and cadences—even the monotonous ones—that go to make up the face of day-to-day baseball. "At its best,"

Tom Wicker of the New York Times says, "baseball unfolds with the grace and precision of the dance."

I do not understand, either, why baseball has to accommodate to the stepped-up tempo of modern, sophisticated life, by introducing a measure of violence into a game that is basically non-violent.

I have never met a fan who journeyed to the ball park to see a batter deprived of his brains by an errant fastball or to see a player unmercifully slashed by flying spikes. I should think people have had more than their share of violence, in the streets and in the senseless martyrdom of their gunned-down heroes. I should think that the sum total of violence sought by fans would be localized in a raucous argument between a spirited manager and an harassed umpire.

I should think, too, as the Hall of Fame historian, Lee Allen, recently pointed out, that many soldiers emerging from the roiled and napalmed villages and jungles of Vietnam, will find baseball a welcome relief. And I should imagine that baseball, whether or not one regards it as the national pastime or the most popular sport, should continue to provide a wonderful counterpoint to the mayhem, sadism and thunder of a half-year of professional football.

In my family my two boys, Steve and Tad, who are 15 and 12, love to play both baseball and football. They love to watch both sports, too. They do not agree that baseball is losing its folk heroes, for they have a special fondness for Mays and Marichal and McLain and Seaver and Brock and even old Ed Charles. At the same time, they are appreciative of the special skills and daring of many of pro football's current stars. A soft spot in the heart for many contemporary baseball players, plus a keen interest in the game's enduring legends and memorabilia is still, it seems to me, a pretty healthy enthusiasm for youngsters. Also, it does not exclude a profound working interest in pro football, the country's current sports obsession.

Perhaps those people who write so critically and negatively about baseball have seen one too many ball games "on the cuff." Perhaps some of them should try taking a youngster to the ball park on a sleepy summer afternoon. Perhaps they might find that baseball, even to the coòl, involved, quick-witted younger generation, is a welcome respite from the unceasing demands of a complex, challenging, fast-changing world.

I'm sure there are ways to cure the decline and fall of the batting average. Many critics have made solid proposals to bring back the base hit. If baseball is wise, which it hasn't always been, it will experiment and search unceasingly to give the batter a better break.

Perhaps the long season *is* too long, perhaps the World Series will be made anti-climactic after doubling the number of pennant races and superimposing divisional playoffs on the regular schedule, for the first time in 1969 (Although I think it will add excitement and a new competitive interest to the sport.) Perhaps some pitchers *do* dawdle unnecessarily, while some batters fidget and fuss too much time away.

But baseball, with all of its warts and imperfections, is still a tranquil, and joyous moment for many, in a brooding and volatile world. As Pulitzer Prize-winning historian, Bruce Cotton, has written, "Baseball will undoubtedly be around for a long time to come. And it will continue, in spite of its own press agents, to be in truth the great American game."

RAY ROBINSON
New York City

DENNY McLAIN

The Rugged Individualist

by RAY ROBINSON

I guess all that's left now to complete the mod mural is a laugh-a-minute Denny McLain joke book, edited by Bill Adler.

Everything else has happened that could happen to this organ-playing, soft drink-swizzling, joyously uninhibited, flap-mouthed baseball vaudevillian: 31 victories and 28 complete games on the mound in 1968; a decisive comeback victory in the sixth game of the World Series after two surprising, ego-numbing defeats at the hands of the Cardinals; a salary somewhere in the $65,000 class; fronting a four-man "combo," as Variety tells us, in a "top coin Las Vegas" date; grabbing The American League Cy Young award and his league's MVP award unanimously.

So now it's gotta be a collection of Denny's happy, crooked-grin quotes. And, you know, he's really a pretty funny guy—for a ballplayer. Maybe he'd be funny even if he wasn't a ballplayer.

Take, for instance, the time he lost the opening game of last year's World Series to Bob Gibson on the Jewish holiday of Yom Kippur.

"I wish I was Jewish after a game like this," said Denny. "Then I wouldn't have had to pitch today."

Or take the time a friend was explaining to Denny how they blamed him for losing the 1967 pennant because he injured his big toe in a curious accident at home and lost five or six key pitching assignments.

"They wanted to run me out of town on a mule,"

11

Denny recalled, "but now they give me a standing ovation for warming up."

Or take the time a friend was explaining to Denny why Detroit fans were so frustrated—prior to their pennant and World Series victory in '68. "They haven't won in 23 years," the friend said.

"That's not *my* fault," said Denny, with a sly grin. "I've been there for only four."

Or take the time somebody had the audacity to boo Denny McLain when he was playing the Hammond organ, which is what he likes to do best, outside of pitch every fourth day and count his money on the fifth.

"Would somebody please shut the parrot up?" requested the muscular Detroit righthander.

Now if you get the notion, from all of this cataloguing of extemporaneous japes, that Dennis Dale McLain, 25, son-in-law of Lou Boudreau, and today baseball's most sizzling show biz property, is nothing more than the pop-off successor to the game's last 30-game winner, Dizzy Dean, you're mightily mistaken. For, in truth, and in anyone's book, including Mayo Smith's, Denny McLain is one heck of a pitcher, even if he is only "an average sort of organist," according to one TV commentator. (Another critic, Dale Stevens of the Detroit *News,* says Denny belongs "somewhere between Toledo and the Three I league" as an organist.)

And you don't have to take his 31 wins in 1968 as sole proof, even if a lot of folks are beginning to suggest that it was all a fluke, that he did it with mirrors and a lot of Tiger run-making behind him.

Look, go back to the three years preceding 1968. In 1965, when Denny was 21, he won 16 and lost only 6, in what was his second full season in the majors. In 1966 he won 20 and lost 14 and in 1967, the year his detractors had him "losing" the flag for Detroit, he won 17 and lost 16. (In '67 he also gave up more homers than any other hurler.)

After some six years of pitching in the big leagues, Denny has 90 wins and 48 defeats. That's a won-loss mark that comes close to a 2-1 ratio of victories over defeats. Pitchers who maintain that type of pace are, to say the least, rare as silent lawyers. Bob Gibson, Don Drysdale and Jim Bunning, other top righthanders of this era, don't come close to such successful performance. Only Juan Marichal, with 170 victories and 77 defeats, has a winning rhythm that excels Denny McLain's.

It remains to be seen, of course, just how Denny McLain faces success. If he becomes surfeited with it, he could, as some insist, become a one-season wonder. Or if he gets his fingers stuck on the keys of his $6,000 X-77 Hammond in the studio of his $80,000 ranch house in Detroit's Farmington suburb, he might have more trouble with the American League batters than he had in 1968.

But if you listen to McLain himself he has little doubts about what the future holds for him and that humming, rising fast ball.

"The difference between me this year (he was talking about his 1968 showing) and the other years is control. Control and concentration. I've just improved myself on the field," insisted McLain. "It's really in knowing what to do. I know the hitters a lot better."

And if anyone thinks Denny McLain will have had all the kicks and kudos one man can reap out of a singular year of baseball magic, he has another big think coming.

"I enjoy the challenge of baseball," says Denny, a thoughtful expression moving over that mischievous choir boy pan. "I always will. You can't visualize the sense of power in pitching when you are good. You sometimes feel as if you can't make a mistake."

There are some keen-eyed observers who have perceptive things to say about what makes Denny run—and, they feel, will continue to make him run, and win.

Johnny Sain, the able Detroit pitching coach, who has had large successes with the Minnesota hurling corps, as well as the Detroit pitching staff, feels McLain became a truly mature pitcher in 1968.

"He has always known what he could do with a baseball," Sain explains, "but now he has learned the technique of doing it correctly. He knows when to throw a rising fastball, instead of a sinking fastball and when to throw a changeup instead of a curve. I think he knows a lot more about what he's doing than the thousands of people in the ball park think he does."

It's interesting that Sain puts his finger on the attitude

of the fans. For Denny's manner, his insouciance, which might be more studied than one suspects, has led some to believe that this baseball original is nothing more than a thrower—maybe the type of big, strong, mouthy guy that Dizzy Dean was in '34 when he started, relieved and bulled his way to 30 wins.

In addition, before his almost unbroken succession of triumphs in '68, the public image of McLain was, in the baseball vernacular, that of the "Super-Flake." Rival managers used to comment negatively about his supposed lack of desire—"his ten-cent attitude," some called it—and it's possible they wouldn't have traded away three banjo hitters and a roll of adhesive tape for him. Bill Rigney, who worries enough about baseball matters to carry around a painful ulcer, took time out from his managing chores with the California Angels, to express his own change of attitude about McLain.

"Once the guy set you to wondering," said Rigney. "But now it looks as if he wants to be a good pitcher. Maybe the best."

But even after he flashed by the 30 mark and went for 31 (he got it against the Yankees on Sept. 19, at Detroit, in a 6-2 win, then lost his bid for No. 32 against the Orioles, 2-1), McLain still refused to change his manner. He wasn't going to become a sober statesman or a solid citizen overnight. If some still preferred to look upon him as an arrogant jock or a cocky kid who sometimes dyed his hair from dirty blond to redhead and back again, that was their business. He would continue to conduct his affairs the way he wanted to. That's what made him Denny McLain, a guy who could tell off the Detroit fans and still listen to 45,000 fans cheering him on the September Saturday when his 5-4 victory over Oakland (seen by millions on nationwide television, as the Game-of-the-Week) gave him the prized 30th.

"We want Denny, We want Denny!" they all yelled and screamed. And he came out of the dugout and waved to his audience, then went in and came out again for still another bow when they refused to let up on the noise. A half hour after the game had become history—precious history to this Chicago kid—McLain was still holding court for the press inside the clubhouse. He loved telling them how he did it and that he was, in his own mind, "a mercenary soldier."

This was Denny McLain to the core. He wouldn't change, simply because he had become only the third pitcher in 50 years to reach the 30-victory crest. Jim Bagby, Sr., of the Cleveland Indians had taken 31 for his team in 1920. Lefty Grove won 31 for Connie Mack's A's in 1931, while losing only four and then, of course, the garrulous Dean had done it in 1934 for the Cards, ending with a 30-7 record.

It was a year when the crowds never stopped singing his praises, when reporters never stopped asking questions, and papers never stopped printing his answers. And through it all Denny was his same mouthy, voluble self.

"Don't be humble," Joe Sparma, a fellow Detroit pitcher, crowed to Denny, one day towards the end of the season. "Don't be humble, Denny, just be yourself!"

It was the same way when Detroit prepared to play the first game of the World Series—its first Series since 1945. The "confrontation" between McLain and the astoundingly talented Bob Gibson had been building tension for three days, following the official ending of the campaign. Of course, this had to be baseball's pitching battle of the century, in a year when pitchers so dominated the game that batters had a hard time getting their names in the papers, not to mention the .300 listings.

So Denny McLain, who once confided to a magazine reporter that his hero was Frank Sinatra because "he doesn't give a damn about anything," kept playing his role to the hilt. He slipped a remark into a pre-game chat that he "was out to humiliate the Cardinals," and even if he didn't say it quite that way, it made good copy and Denny went along with it. When he heard that some rancorous Card strategist had posted the remark on the St. Louis bulletin board, Denny professed not to be upset in the least.

Then he went out on the eve of battle with Gibson and sat down in the lobby of a downtown St. Louis hotel and gave an impromptu organ recital. He played mood music like "Stardust," then breezed into some rock-and-roll tempos. This was Denny the extrovert. The audience loved it—and so did he.

The next afternoon he faced Gibson—and didn't make it past the fifth inning.

He didn't make it in the second Gibson-McLain duel, either, in Game 4. Lou Brock drove Denny's second pitch of the afternoon some 460 feet away, into the upper deck in Detroit's right-center field.

After that Denny struggled, but with little success. His arm, tired and sore after the long season, wasn't up to it, for the second straight time against Gibson.

Following the loss, McLain sounded like he might be through for the Series and the season. His arm throbbed with pain. But when the Tigers won the fifth game and marched back into contention, Denny took a shot in the arm from Dr. Russell Wright's needle, told Manager Smith he was ready to do battle again, and, with the help of a thunderous Detroit attack in Game 6, he evened the Series at three games each. The good overhand curve had come back. The 30-game pitch had returned.

If there is a single thing that has ruffled the calm in the McLain household, after such a year of achievement and glory, it is the suspicion, on Sharyn McLain's part, that her husband is regarded as a somewhat tough-hearted eccentric.

Nothing could be further from the truth, insists Sharyn. The man is really a softie, a guy who gets nervous before he pitches, she says.

"If Denny were as hard as the press makes him out to be," says Lou Boudreau's daughter, "he never could have adopted a child." She was referring to Dennis, who is now little more than a year old.

And is her gabby husband an Alibi Ike?

Not on your life.

"If he loses a ball game," says Sharyn, "he comes home, sits down at the organ and plays, maybe for an hour or two. Then it's all over. He never brings home any excuses."

One gets the feeling Denny McLain won't need any excuses for 1969, either. Take it from Dizzy Dean himself that McLain might go on to new heights of 35 wins this year!

"With the league goin' to 12 teams," says Dean, "all the clubs will be weaker."

That'll make McLain stronger.

RAY ROBINSON has edited Baseball Stars since 1958. He is the articles Editor of Good Housekeeping and the author of a half-dozen books on sports.

DENNY McLAIN

Year	Club	Lea	IP	W	L	SO	BB	H	ERA
1962	Harlan	Appal.	18	1	1	32	10	9	0.00
1962	Clinton	Midwest	91	4	7	93	37	92	3.56
1963	Duluth-Superior	Northern	141	13	2	157	51	117	2.55
1963	Knoxville	So. Atl.	77	5	4	82	28	61	3.51
1963	Detroit	A. L.	21	2	1	22	16	20	4.29
1964	Syracuse	Int.	59	3	1	56	18	38	1.53
1964	Detroit	A. L.	100	4	5	70	37	84	4.05
1965	Detroit	A. L.	220	16	6	192	62	174	2.62
1966	Detroit	A. L.	264	20	14	192	104	205	3.92
1967	Detroit	A. L.	235	17	16	161	73	209	3.79
1968	Detroit	A. L.	336	31	6	279	63	180	1.93
World Series									
1968	Detroit	A. L.	16⅔	1	2	13	4	18	3.18

BOB GIBSON

Best Ever?

by IRA PECK

If 1968 was the year of the pitcher (and the statistics seem to prove that it was), then the pitcher of the year just had to be Bob Gibson of the St. Louis Cardinals. Not that Gibson won 30 or 31 games. He didn't. He didn't even win 25, although he might easily have won more than that if Cardinal bats hadn't turned to Jello almost every time Gibson took the hill last summer. Gibson "only" won 22 games while losing nine. If that doesn't seem particularly astonishing, consider these additional statistics compiled by Gibson:

An earned run average of 1.12 per game. Thirteen shutouts. Twenty-eight complete games in 34 starts. A total of 268 strikeouts in 305 innings.

Now we'll take a closer look at that 1.12 ERA and try to put it into some perspective. To do that, let's try a little quiz:

Which of the following pitchers of recent years had a better one-season ERA?

a) Sandy Koufax b) Juan Marichal c) Warren Spahn d) Don Drysdale e) none of these

If your answer was "e," you were right.

Now let's go back a generation or so to the 1930's, when, many fans insist, baseball reached a peak of excellence.

Which of the following pitchers of the 1930's had a better one-season ERA than Gibson's 1.12?

a) Lefty Grove b) Dizzy Dean c) Carl Hubbell d) Bob Feller e) none of these

If your answer was "e," you were right again.

Want to go back even further—to the dead-ball era of Walter Johnson, Grover Cleveland Alexander or even Christy Mathewson? Forget it. The answer would still be the same. *Nobody, but nobody* ever had a better one-season ERA than 1.12 since baseball records have been kept. Before Gibson set that mark last year, the best previous record was Walter Johnson's 1.14 set in 1913 in the American League. The best previous mark in the National League was Alexander's 1.22 set in 1915.

How did Gibson, a fireballing right-hander, manage to achieve his historic mark? Easy. During one stretch of the season, Bob won 15 straight games. Included in that stretch were 92 consecutive innings in which he allowed exactly two (2) runs, one on a wild pitch. Red Schoendienst, the Cardinals' manager, may be prejudiced, of course, but he said at that time:

"Nobody has ever pitched better than Bob Gibson."

Less biased observers than Schoendienst have conceded that Bob's 1968 season was, in many ways, the best quality season of any pitcher in baseball history.

So that puts Gibson right up there among the pitching gods, doesn't it? It sure does. And, if you're trying to figure out how on earth Gibson ever lost nine games in 1968, the answer is simple. The Cardinals had a distressing habit of scoring one, or zero runs when Bob pitched. There was one game in which Bob gave up exactly one hit in eight innings. The hit, unfortunately, was a double that scored a run. So Bob was behind 1-0 (again) and was taken out for a pinch-hitter in the bottom of the eighth. The Cards didn't score, anyway, their relief pitcher gave up a run in the ninth, and the final score was 2-0. Losing pitcher, Bob Gibson. Perhaps Bob pitched 13 shutouts in 1968 because it was the only way he could guarantee himself of at least a tie in those games.

So Bob Gibson joined the pitching immortals (he was the unanimous selection for the NL Cy Young award and also the Most Valuable Player, only the seventh time in the history of the award it has gone to a pitcher). In the process, he pitched the Cardinals to their second straight pennant and World Series. Bob had already pitched heroically against the Boston Red Sox in the 1967 World Series, winning three of the four Cardinal victories.

Among other things, Bob gave up just 14 hits in those three (complete) games, tying the record set by Christy Mathewson of the New York Giants in 1905. And in the 1964 World Series, against the New York Yankees, Bob had won two of the Cardinals four victories and set a series record for strikeouts with 31.

So here it is, October 1968, another World Series, and what do you do for an encore? Well, for openers, Bob set a new World Series record by striking out 17 Detroit batters as he won the first game, 4-0. This game was supposed to be the pitching duel of the century, with Gibson pitted against 31-game winner Denny McLain of the Tigers. It didn't turn out that way. McLain was lifted after pitching five innings and giving up three runs. Nevertheless, there was tremendous drama in this game, drama that Gibson himself was not even aware of for the most part.

Going into the ninth inning, Gibson had struck out 14 men. He needed just one more to tie Sandy Koufax's record of 15. Apparently, Gibson was the only one in the ball park (Attendance—54,692) who didn't know it. The Cardinal ballplayers knew it, but they weren't telling him— you know, it's bad luck. The fans in the stands knew it, because they'd heard it on their transistor radios. Only Bob Gibson didn't know it. So, as Gibson started the ninth inning, the fans were all pulling for him to break Sandy Koufax's record, and there was Gibson, oblivious to it all. The fans kept rooting for foul balls to fall into the stands, and not into the gloves of Cardinal fielders. Each time a Tiger batter popped a ball into the air, the fans would instinctively twist their bodies in the direction of the stands, hoping to put enough "English" on the ball to steer it out of play. They didn't want to see pop foul-outs. They wanted to see strikeouts. They wanted to see Bob Gibson make history.

Gibson didn't let them down. After Mickey Stanley singled, Bob struck out Al Kaline, tying Koufax's mark. Gibson seemed startled when the crowd rose and gave him a standing ovation. Then the news was flashed on the scoreboard and Gibson was finally let in on the secret. He remained unaware, however, of the fans' body gyrations as he struck out the next two men (two more standing ovations) to break the record and end the game. For the sake of history, the two men were Norm Cash and Willie Horton. Later Bob said he hadn't noticed all the body English in the stands. You don't see those things from the field, he said, and besides he was just interested in getting outs, any kind.

So now it was the fourth game of the Series, the Cardinals were ahead two games to one, and Gibson was on the mound again for St. Louis. Or he was whenever the rain that day permitted. The game was held up for 37 minutes at the start, and again for 74 minutes in the third inning. The delays had to put an additional strain on the 32-year-old right-hander's arm. So what did Gibson do? Well, for one thing, he won 10-1, giving up just five hits and striking out 10 men. It was Gibson's seventh consecutive World Series victory, and a new record. And Gibson added a bit of spice to it by clouting a home run, his second World Series four-bagger, and a record for a pitcher.

The Tigers came back strongly to take the fifth and sixth games, and now it was the seventh and final game of the 1968 World Series. And again Bob Gibson was on the mound and, for St. Louis fans, that was money in the bank, wasn't it? For six-and-two-thirds innings, it looked like it. In that stretch, Gibson gave up just one hit, an infield single, and no runs. The only fly in the ointment was that the Cardinals hadn't scored any runs off Tiger pitcher Mickey Lolich either, although they had managed four hits. Then, with two out in the top of the seventh, Gibson, the almost-perfect pitcher, faltered. He gave up consecutive well-hit singles to Norm Cash and Willie Horton. The next man up, Jim Northrup, hit a long drive to center field. Curt Flood, the almost-perfect center-fielder, misjudged the ball. He took three steps in, stopped, slipped slightly, and then headed back to the wall. It was too late. The ball sailed over his outstretched glove and rolled to the wall. It went for a triple, and scored two runs. They were all Lolich needed. The final score was Detroit 4, St. Louis 1, and the Tigers had won the World Series.

Gibson, who doesn't like to lose, was bitter after the game, but made no alibis. He said he had felt somewhat tired pitching with three days rest for the second time in the Series. In the regular season, he normally pitches with four days between starts.

"You're bound to go downhill if you keep pitching on two or three days rest," he said. "You don't get better. But only two days of rest didn't seem to bother Lolich today. I thought I pitched all right today. We just didn't get any runs."

But Bob wasn't bitter about his roommate Curt Flood's goof in the seventh inning. "Curt said it was his fault," Gibson recalled, "and I said, 'no it isn't.' What else can you say?"

There was, however, plenty of consolation for Gibson personally in the Series. When all the statistics were in, Bob had set six new World Series records. Among them, his 35 strikeouts topped his old mark of 31, set against the Yankees in 1964.

If Gibson was bitter about defeat, he was even more bitter about some of the mail he had gotten during the series—hate mail. One of the letters included this gem: "Why don't you and the other blackbirds on the Cardinals move to Africa where you belong?" Letters like that upset Gibson plenty, as does every other manifestation of prejudice and bigotry toward his race. Ironically, they help to make him a better pitcher. Prejudice, which he has experienced all his life, has made him fiercely combative, both on and off the field. One ballplayer put it rather succinctly: "Some pitchers," he said, load the ball with spit. Others"—meaning Gibson—"load it with anger."

Bob Gibson was born November 9, 1935, in an Omaha ghetto. His father, a mill worker, died of pneumonia just before Bob was born. His mother worked in a laundry and as a cleaning woman to raise her seven children. Bob, the youngest child, was a sickly kid, experiencing pneumonia, asthma, hay fever, rickets and a rheumatic heart at an early age. By the time he was 10, however, he had grown sturdy, and an older brother, Josh, who worked with the local YMCA, coached him in sports. Bob was too skinny to play football in high school, but he did play basketball and baseball, and made the track squad, too. Bob hoped to win a basketball scholarship to Indiana University, but he was informed that Indiana had already met its quota of Negro athletic scholarships. (Later Bob learned that the Negro quota was one.) It was his first real taste of discrimination in sports.

Bob did win a basketball scholarship to Creighton University in Omaha, and became the first Negro to play varsity basketball and baseball there. If Bob had any illusions about not having to study, he was soon disillusioned. In his excellent autobiography, *From Ghetto to Glory,* Bob recalled:

"Creighton is run by the Jesuit fathers, who are dedicated to the old-fashioned idea that the reason for going to college is to study. They stay on your back all the time. It didn't matter if you were a basketball player or not. You had to keep up your grades or else you found yourself out on the street where all your press clippings couldn't help you."

After his freshman year, Bob knuckled down to his studies to the satisfaction of the Jesuit fathers—and himself.

At Creighton, Bob played center field and also pitched occasionally for the baseball team. In 1957, the Cardinals signed him to a contract that called for a $4,000 bonus, and assigned him to their AAA farm club in Omaha. Bob's manager was the late Johnny Keane, a patient, fatherly, little man who was great with young ballplayers. Keane had no idea where Gibson belonged on a ball field, but one day he asked him to pitch batting practice half-speed. Nobody hit a ball out of the batting cage. "Throw some curves," Keane shouted. Gibson didn't have a curve then, but he had a slider, and he threw it. Nobody hit one of his sliders out of the cage either. Keane was watching Gibson intently. "Should I start throwing hard?" Gibson asked ingenuously. Keane laughed. "No," he said. "That's fine." From that day on, Gibson was a pitcher.

Bob didn't burn up the minors at first, but he kept improving, and in 1958 he was invited to spring training with the Cardinals. Bob couldn't wait. Checking in at the Cardinals' hotel in St. Petersburg, Florida, he told the desk clerk proudly, "My name is Bob Gibson. I'm with the St. Louis Cardinal ball club. You're supposed to have a room for me." The desk clerk gave him a fishy look, and then handed him an address. It was, of course, in the Negro ghetto and to Bob it was a bitter experience. "So this is the major leagues," he said to himself.

The next two years, Bob shuttled back and forth in the Cardinal farm system, with an occasional shot at the parent club. By 1960, he was in St. Louis to stay. But life was far from sweet even then. Bob's manager was Solly Hemus, an aggressive man who had little patience with his young pitcher. He was prone to humiliate Gibson before the other players by calling him a "thrower" rather than a pitcher. And he pitched Gibson only infrequently. It was hardly the kind of treatment to instill confidence in a young pitcher. Bob wasn't very heartbroken when Hemus was fired in the middle of the 1961 season. His new manager was a man he liked and respected, Johnny Keane. The day Keane took over, he handed Gibson a ball. "You're pitching tonight, Hoot," he said softly. "And from now on you're in the regular rotation." To Bob, it was like being let out of jail.

From then on, Bob kept getting better. He won 13 games in 1961, 15 in 1962, 18 in 1963, 19 in 1964, 20 in 1965, 21 in 1966. A broken leg suffered in the 1967 season kept Bob from winning more than 13, but he came back strongly last year to win 22.

What kind of a guy is Bob Gibson? He's outspoken, especially where prejudice is concerned, honest to the point of being blunt, especially when reporters ask him "silly" questions and, above all, has a world of courage. Perhaps the best example of his competitive spirit and raw courage took place in the seventh game of the 1964 World Series against the Yankees. Bob was pitching with only two days rest, and anyone who saw the game on TV will remember how he was panting, even gasping for breath after the sixth inning. In the ninth inning, the Cardinals, who had once held a 6-0 lead, were still ahead, 7-5. But Bob was being shelled hard, and it looked like the Yankees might come from behind and win. Johnny Keane walked out to the mound.

"How do you feel, Hoot?" he asked.

Bob was exhausted, as Keane undoubtedly knew, but he said, "I feel fine." Bob explained his feelings at the time in his book, *From Ghetto to Glory:*

"I wouldn't have cared if I was keeling over out there, I never would say I was tired. You never feel you're not the right guy to do the job unless you're hurt. It goes with having confidence in yourself. You could be out on your feet and they could be beating your brains out, and you still think you're the best and you can get them out. This is the feeling you have to have. Very few guys give up, and that's what you'd be doing if you told the manager you were tired; you would be giving up. It's very seldom that a manager takes your word anyway. He knows what he wants to do when he comes out there and Keane wanted me to stay."

As Bob expected, Keane told him, "I want you to finish this."

Bob then got the last man out (it was Bobby Richardson) and the Cardinals were world champions. Later a reporter asked Keane why he had stuck with Gibson when he was so obviously tired and the Yankees were threatening.

Keane said, "I was committed to his heart. Bob is a real thoroughbred."

Nobody ever said it better.

IRA PECK, the author of a new book, "The Life and Words of Martin Luther King, Jr.," is a lifetime Cardinal fan, who thinks the Cards will make it three-in-a-row this year.

BOB GIBSON

Year	Club	Lea	IP	W	L	SO	BB	H	ERA
1957	Omaha	A. A.	42	2	1	25	27	46	4.29
1957	Columbus	So. Atl.	43	4	3	24	34	36	3.77
1958	Omaha	A. A.	87	3	4	47	39	79	3.31
1958	Rochester	Int.	103	5	5	75	54	88	2.45
1959	Omaha	A. A.	135	9	9	98	70	128	3.07
1959	St. Louis	N. L.	76	3	5	48	39	77	3.32
1960	Rochester	Int.	41	2	3	36	17	33	2.85
1960	St. Louis	N. L.	87	3	6	69	48	97	5.59
1961	St. Louis	N. L.	211	13	12	166	119	186	3.24
1962	St. Louis	N. L.	234	15	13	208	95	174	2.85
1963	St. Louis	N. L.	255	18	9	204	96	224	3.39
1964	St. Louis	N. L.	287	19	12	245	86	250	3.01
1965	St. Louis	N. L.	299	20	12	270	103	243	3.07
1966	St. Louis	N. L.	280	21	12	225	78	210	2.44
1967	St. Louis	N. L.	175	13	7	147	40	151	2.98
1968	St. Louis	N. L.	304	22	9	268	62	198	1.12
World Series									
1964	St. Louis	N. L.	27	2	1	31	8	22	3.00
1967	St. Louis	N. L.	27	3	0	26	5	14	1.00
1968	St. Louis	N. L.	27	2	1	35	4	18	1.67

LOU BROCK

"A Walk Is a Two-Bagger"

by RAY ROBINSON

If you're still wondering why Louis Clark Brock, the 29-year-old terrier from El Dorado, Arkansas, had such a bad 1968 World Series, it's simply because he had a sore right knee encapped in a fabric brace and a petulant right shoulder that pestered him when he slid.

Now do you understand why the man did so poorly? Now do you understand why he could only finish up with a .464 batting average and seven stolen bases? Now do you understand why the Cards couldn't win it—and the Tigers couldn't lose it?

Well, all of this verbiage is sort of a nasty little joke, for Lou Brock had one heck of a Series, in spite of injuries, real, illusory and otherwise. Or let's say he had one-half of a great World Series. For four games, if you will turn your mind back to this little fellow's amazing demonstration, he was so good that he had the opposition screaming for mercy—quietly, that is, when they were home with their wives.

Even Red Smith, the nationally syndicated columnist, who is not given to unnecessary hyperbole, wrote one day, after Lou registered three hits, including a double, triple and homer, four runs batted in, two runs scored and one stolen base, that "there is no power on earth that can keep Brock from making a joke of this game." There happened to be such a power—and it turned out to be a round-bellied lefty named Mickey Lolich, who found a way to get Lou Brock out, at least on the bases, in games five and seven.

When he did, that was the Series—and that was the end of the Cardinals. With seven steals in the first four games and a .524 batting average after five games, Lou Brock had everybody, including eyewitness Casey Stengel, mumbling and stuttering in disbelief. "Not even the photographers can catch him with those long lenses," exaggerated the phrase-popping, ex-Yankee manager. Sandy Koufax, covering the Series for NBC, said, in his quiet way: "A truly remarkable little man, with surprising power."

The fact is that Lou Brock reminds me of my son, Tad, who plays ball on a dirty city street with the same abandon that Brock exhibits on the wonderfully manicured lawns of the majors. Lou is like an insouciant boy, playing with delicious desire and joyous bounce. Watch Lou as he leads off first base (he stole 62 bases in 1968, double the amount turned in by the entire Detroit team), his tongue darting from one side of his mouth to the other, his eyes alertly watching the pitcher and the first baseman, inevitably picking up every tell-tale move. Then he goes, confident, totally involved. ("I don't believe," he says, "that I can be thrown out stealing second base if I get the proper jump on the pitcher. If they pitch out on me, most of the time I can anticipate the pitchout.")

Why, in the first half of the 1968 Series Lou Brock made Pepper Martin, of 1931 Series glory, look like a water-logged buffalo. He made Bill Freehan, billed as the American League's best catcher, look like a helpless plumber called in to halt a sea-tide.

What is the essence of Lou Brock, who in eight big-league years since 1961, first with the Chicago Cubs, then with the Cards, has become baseball's most exciting ballplayer? Once it was Willie Mays, a slugger, sparkling base-runner and a superior fielder, who won hands down the nomination as the game's best all-around performer. But now you won't hear a word of dissent, in either league, if Lou is acclaimed as Willie's legitimate successor.

There have been some accusations that Brock is a "hot dog." But these cries invariably arise from those who have been victimized by this 168-pound scrambler. For instance, there were ugly little rumors during the last World Series that Mickey Lolich, supposedly burned up by Lou's three steals against him in a second game that seemed beyond the Cards grasp, regarded Lou's actions as nothing but a manifestation of self-seeking. "He's doing it for records, self-glory," was the way one writer quoted Mickey. Later, Mickey insisted he said no such thing. What's more, Lolich said, he had phoned Brock to tell him he'd never downgraded him in any such fashion.

Brock, who had run and stolen on Lolich with his club five runs behind, certainly an unorthodox and unexpected maneuver, explained that that's the way he plays the game. "It's worth the gamble," he said. "We are a club that scratches for runs. I run to stay out of double-play situations. If we play it safe, that's not the Cardinals. If you decide to give up the game because you are five or six runs behind, what's the use of playing it out?"

Those who play and think about this game by the book may regard this theory as wrong-headed. To those who prefer to regard baseball as a game in which nothing is truly decided until 27 outs have been registered against the loser, it is perfectly sound operating procedure. Especially if your name is Lou Brock and you have the heart and desire to play the game that way.

"This guy," says Joe Garagiola, the former big-league catcher, who has become the Jimmy Breslin of broadcasters, "has an inner conceit, an arrogance. There are other players who probably can lick him in a straight race. But on those bases he's the best. I guess the only way to stop him is to sneak into the clubhouse and burn his spikes."

Garagiola must have had in mind the fact that Brock, on several occasions with the Cards, has scored all the way from second base on a puny infield bunt.

Earl Wilson, the Detroit pitcher who faced Brock in only one game in the Series, is also Lou's pal off the field. But he knows and appreciates the fact that Lou would run on his arthritic grandmother.

"Sure, I know he'll run on me," said Earl during the Series. "Just let him reach base."

From the point of view of the catcher, the man who usually gets blamed for stolen bases, though it is unwise to eliminate the pitcher from major blame for such swindles, Brock is simply a scandal. Freehan, the big Detroit man in the mask, knew Lou had made him look ragged in the first four games.

"He unnerves guys," admitted Freehan. "I don't think we have anyone in our league who dares the pitcher the way he does. He tries to force you to make mistakes by hurrying things up. That's his bag."

Despite his letdown in the last three games of the Series (a letdown, of course, that was only relative, based on the impossibility of competing against his earlier performance), Brock came away from a losing Series with an increased reputation.

"I think he's the best I've ever seen," said Yankee manager Ralph Houk. And Mike Shannon, Lou's hard-working teammate, emerged with the witty assessment of the classic, when he said, "When Lou gets a base on balls, that's a two-base walk." Considering the statistics he has run up, with a personal season high of 74 stolen bases with the Cards in 1966, Brock seems to merit such rating. He has now stolen 334 bases in his major-league career, aside from the 14 steals in three Series (he surprisingly failed to steal a single base in 1964 against the Yanks, when he batted .300), and has been shot down 111 times.

Once, in comparing Brock with Maury Wills, who set an all-time record in 1962 of 104 stolen bases when he worked for the Los Angeles Dodgers, Stan Musial stated a simple truth. "Lou can do more things."

There is little doubt about this. Wills has always been a poke hitter, a Punch and Judy. Brock can hit that way, too. But he can also hit with power. He hit 21 homers in 1967 and, in 1962, before they tore down the ancient Polo Grounds in New York to make way for a housing project, he became as famous as Willie Mays in the area by being one of only two human beings ever to cow-tail a ball into the distant center-field bleachers. The other guy who did it was Joe Adcock, who, after a respectable evening at the dinner table, weighed about 60 pounds more than Brock. Though he is a leadoff man, Brock bats in runs; last year he knocked across 51, the year before he had 76.

In the field Lou is no Curt Flood—but he still covers his position as well as most of them. Last year, however, he made 14 errors, tying him with Alex Johnson of the Reds for most miscues by an NL outfielder.

Brock's teammates like to see him get on to start a game. They should. It's an omen of better things to come. The fans like it, too. It means action, excitement; everyone and everything comes alive, even the butterflies in the enemy pitcher's stomach.

Ironically, the man who today is baseball's most stimulating player, was traded off by the Cubs to the Cards in mid-season of 1964, simply because the Chicagoans didn't have the vision of Mr. Magoo. The men involved in the deal that brought Lou to St. Lou—pitcher Ernie Broglio, pitcher Bobby Shantz, outfielder Doug Clemens, all of whom went to the Windy City—were washouts. Shantz, a courageous lefty with many skills, had had his best years. Broglio continued to be a disappointment. Clemens had always been a journeyman. One has to wonder sometimes about the miraculous machinations of baseball front offices.

Most people feel that Brock's arrival with the Cards helped to give Manager Johnny Keane a pennant in '64. Lou ended the year with 200 hits—and most of 'em (144) were carved in Keane's behalf. He also had 43 stolen bases and a BA of .315, still his highest big-time mark. When he left the Cubs Lou had been hitting .251; with the Cards he hit .348.

"I was a greenhorn with the Cubs," Lou once told sportswriter Maury Allen of the *New York Post*. "I was learning the game with them. I had more opportunity to show what I had with the Cards."

He was right. The first day Lou arrived in St. Louis, manager Keane walked him out to left field and told him "this is all yours. We know you can do it all. We're going to stay with you."

In the mold of many major leaguers today, Brock is articulate, quick-witted and curious about matters that have nothing to do with the game that he plays so zealously. One of nine children, Lou attended Southern University in Baton Rouge, Louisiana, where he did nicely in mathematics and thought of becoming an architectural engineer. As a student he was more interested in track, until he discovered his baseball talents.

He has worked in the off-season as a salesman and now owns a florist business in the Clayton neighborhood of St. Louis. The man who is now tied at 14 with Eddie Collins, the all-time second baseman of the White Sox and A's, for most World Series stolen bases and shares a record 13-hit total for a seven-game Series with New York's Bobby Richardson, has come a long way from his Arkansas beginnings.

Now he even speaks to his country's political celebrities. While he was bombarding the Tigers in the first four games, Brock had a visitor in the St. Louis clubhouse. It was a man named Hubert Humphrey.

"If I could run as fast as you, I'd be in," Mr. Humphrey told Lou Brock.

"Thank you," said Lou, "and good luck."

That was a few hours before Lou Brock's own good luck slipped away in '68.

LOU BROCK

Year	Club	Lea	Pos	AB	R	H	HR	RBI	Avg
1961	St. Cloud	Northern	OF	501	117	181	14	82	.361
1961	Chicago	N. L.	OF	11	1	1	0	0	.091
1962	Chicago	N. L.	OF	434	73	114	9	35	.263
1963	Chicago	N. L.	OF	547	79	141	9	37	.258
1964	Chi.-St. Louis	N. L.	OF	634	111	200	14	58	.315
1965	St. Louis	N. L.	OF	631	107	182	16	69	.288
1966	St. Louis	N. L.	OF	643	94	183	15	46	.285
1967	St. Louis	N. L.	OF	689	113	206	21	76	.299
1968	St. Louis	N. L.	OF	660	92	184	6	51	.279
World Series									
1964	St. Louis	N. L.	OF	30	2	9	1	5	.300
1967	St. Louis	N. L.	OF	29	8	12	1	3	.414
1968	St. Louis	N. L.	OF	28	6	13	2	5	.464

WILLIE MAYS

Next Stop: 600 Homers

by BILL LIBBY

He is still there now, as it seems he has always been, swinging hard, so hard the bat wrenches out of his right hand. He follows through one-handed, popping up or hitting the ball up into the outfield seats, running hard, so hard his cap flies off, drifting effortlessly under a fly ball and making his trademark "basket catch," letting the ball drop into his glove at his belly. He is still there, in center field for the Giants, and sometimes it seems not so much has changed.

When was it he came up now, 1951? "Oh my," Willie Mays smiles wistfully, "sure was a long time ago." Sure was. That was in New York and now he has completed seventeen seasons in the major leagues, the last eleven of them in San Francisco. It seems like only yesterday that he was sparking the Giants to that "miracle" pennant of '51 that lit up the old Polo Grounds. But the old Polo Grounds is gone now, and they just dedicated a softball field there to him—softball?—and Mays has passed more than a decade in Candlestick Park.

He still has a boyish face and a boyish grin, but you can see he is no boy any more now, when you look at him. His pipsqueak voice, endlessly yelling, "Say, hey," in the old days, has deepened, and he speaks softly and thoughtfully now. He does not play with quite the same abandon, with the youthful enthusiasm that was so captivating in the early years. It is a struggle for him now, for he has been sick and injured a lot in recent seasons, and he gets tired now. He will be 38 years old in May.

"I got to play as much as I can, because the big guys are supposed to play," he says. "The other guys, especially the kids, they have to know I won't dog it. But it gets harder every year. I try to play when I shouldn't sometimes, but a couple of times I took myself out, too." He shakes his head. "They say the old guys in the old days had it harder and were tougher, but I got to think they're wrong. They didn't play night and twilight and everything else, day games after night games. They didn't travel coast to coast. They weren't always getting off of planes at some airport at four o'clock in the morning."

Year before last was the worst, 141 games, which isn't bad, but which was the fewest he'd played since he was a kid. But last year, not as troubled by illness and injury, he came back and played 148 games, most of them full-time, missing only 14 full games. He had driven in 100 or more runs eight straight seasons up until 1967. Now, with last year, he has failed two straight seasons. Yet in a year of pitching predominance, Mays' figures weren't bad—a .289 batting average, 20 doubles, 23 homers, 79 runs driven in, 84 scored, 19 games won for the Giants with game-winning hits. He even stole a dozen bases, which is nothing like the 40 he stole in his peak season, but is a lot for an old ballplayer.

There are times he gets discouraged. After a game in which he had struck out a couple of times, he sagged on a stool in the dressing room, his sweaty and soiled uniform stripped off and piled at his feet, his dark skin moist, his taut muscles quivering, and he said, "These kid pitchers— they're all so strong and throw the ball so hard they make you feel too old too soon."

He is not as indomitable as he used to be, standing in there against wild pitchers and brush-back specialists and banging the ball. He bails out now, sometimes.

Once, not so long ago, after a Chicago kid pitcher named Bill Faul had sent him sprawling in the dirt, Willie wanted his pitcher, Juan Marichal, to knock down the Cub star, Ernie Banks. Marichal did not. On the bench, Mays asked Marichal why he hadn't. Marichal said, "Banks is a nice guy."

Mays shrugged and said, "Well, so am I."

He says, very seriously, "I got to be protected. I tell that to all my pitchers."

He is, even now, a key man on the Giants, a team that seems to finish second every season and finished second again last season. The fans seem tired of second-place finishes. It no longer impresses them. They have had only one pennant and that was back in 1962. The Giants were not even contenders last season, despite their second-place finish. There was literally no pennant race. The fans now ridicule Candlestick Park, which is too cold and windy and has gotten too old too soon. Last season, for the first time since they moved to San Francisco, the Giants drew less than a million fans. They had competition from Oakland across the Bay and pulled just 837,220 persons to their ball park.

Mays and the great slugger Willie McCovey and the great pitcher, Juan Marichal, who works practically every fourth day, are the only established stars and attractive performers on the team these days. Jim Ray Hart is a good ballplayer, but now it seems he will not ever be quite as good as most thought he would be. Gaylord Perry has his days. There are a few promising kids. But now you have to wonder, when Mays goes, what will become of the Giants? He is the Giants, as much as Christy Mathewson or Mel Ott were in their days.

Late last season, Mays sat in the dugout in the twilight watching the fans trickle into the arena, watching the other players, almost every single one of them younger than he, kidding around in pre-game batting practice, and he said, "I don't know how many more years. I get asked everywhere I go, all the time, and I don't know what to tell 'em because I don't know myself. Two or three more maybe. One maybe. None maybe. If the mood strikes me," he grinned. "I don't think it will. I hate to think of not playing. But I'm gettin' there. Some days these days, I hate to think of playing," he admitted.

And what happens when he is through playing? "Maybe they'll make me president of the league," Mays smiled. "Or a vice-president of the Giants, like Stan Musial of the Cardinals. Or maybe manager," he said, still smiling. "Or coach. Or maybe I'll leave the game and become president of a bank or something, or maybe just sit around home counting my money."

He has the money to count, since he has been making $125,000 a year the last few years, and since he straightened himself out financially. About five years ago, he had blown a bundle and was broke and in debt, but Jacob Shemano, president of Golden Gate National Bank, took a friendly interest in Mays and helped him get his affairs in order.

But sit around home? Possibly, but it is lonely there. Mays lives alone in a $100,000, three-level, nine-room house on a hill overlooking the Golden Gate Bridge. He is divorced. He likes to have his son with him a lot, but otherwise he seems to have few close friends. He doesn't seem to date a whole lot. He doesn't go out a lot. He is something of a loner.

He has never worked at a single job outside of baseball in his life. Born in Westfield, Alabama, raised in Birmingham, Willie's father was a pullman porter. "He made pretty good tips and he always gave me my walking-around money," Willie says. At 12, he became a playing bat boy for the Birmingham Black Barons, who shared equally with the other players when they passed the hat through the stands. At 19, he had signed with the Giants and begun a minor-league apprenticeship that lasted only 116 games and into the second season. At 20, he was with the Giants and in the majors to stay.

There was a time no one could have imagined Willie Mays as a major-league manager, but that time has passed. When he was named captain of the Giants in 1964, he became the first Negro ever accorded that honor. Alvin Dark, then the manager of the Giants, said, "Mays is a leader without opening his mouth." Harvey Kuenn, who at that time was considered the Giants' leader, said, "Everybody respects Mays—not only as a great player, but as a man."

People began to regard Mays' managerial potential more closely. Under manager Herman Franks, Mays was allowed to exercise considerable influence on the club, especially on the younger players. Former Giant Monte Irvin said, "Willie is mellowed and more mature than he used to be. He feels that his role as captain of the Giants had added stature and dignity to him. He feels it has given him responsibility. He has become an advisor. And someday he wants to apply his leadership skill to the challenge of managing in the majors."

Mays shrugs and says, "It would be a challenge. But it's

a tough job, without much security. So is coaching, which pays even less. Anyway, I don't know if I could get it if I wanted it."

The times are changing, but not as fast as some think. There have been few Negro managers or head coaches in all of professional sports so far, with Bill Russell of the Boston basketball team a notable exception.

In 1951, six years after Jackie Robinson signed a contract as the first Negro player in organized baseball, Sam Bankhead became the first Negro manager in the game with a Canadian team in the Provincial League. There have been others since and some Negro coaches, even in the majors, beginning with Buck O'Neill of the Chicago Cubs in 1962, but there has not yet been a Negro manager in major-league baseball.

Some feel the barrier will be broken eventually, but not by Mays. Among current Negro major leaguers, Maury Wills, Elston Howard, now a Yank coach, Hank Aaron and Bill White have been prominently mentioned as individuals capable of managing in the majors.

Some feel Mays has not been sufficiently active as a leader of his race. Brad Pye, an influential journalist with the Los Angeles *Sentinel*, a major Negro newspaper, once told us, "The first Negro manager will have to be exceptional, admired not only by whites, but also by Negroes. He will have to overcome special problems whenever he benches a player, say, or has to step on one. Mays has played by instinct. He never had to learn. I doubt that he can teach. He has not campaigned for Civil Rights. I doubt that he could lead Negroes across the street. And if he can't lead Negroes, he can't lead whites."

Maury Wills applied publicly for a managerial post last summer, feeling the four new expansion clubs, which needed managers, posed a unique opportunity for a prominent Negro star. When a job failed to materialize, he admitted, "I'm deeply disappointed. Now I have to feel there will not be a Negro manager for a long time, until long after my time has passed."

Many felt Mays lost his chance when Clyde King was signed to replace the retiring Franks last October as manager of the Giants. King was groomed in the Giant system and was regarded highly, but many thought the

Giants, sagging at the gate, might go to Mays as the new mentor. Possibly they will yet, a year from now or two years from now, if King does not fare well in what shapes up as the difficult task of rebuilding the club.

Baseball is not noted for its sentiment, but most presume the Giants will wish to retain the splendid image of Mays even after his playing days end. Perhaps he is not a central figure in the black drive for equality. "I'm not a politician," he shrugs. But he remains well-regarded by most, he has not been seriously soiled by scandal and he is a symbol of much that is best and most exciting about the game.

Entering his 18th season in the major leagues, he has a career batting average of .308. He has hit 587 home runs, second only to Babe Ruth's 714 in big-league history, and when Willie reaches the round figure of 600 during 1969, as he almost certainly will, there should be a colorful ceremony.

He is sixth on the all-time list with 5,277 total bases, seventh with 1,162 extra-base hits, and nearing the top ten with 1,654 RBI's. He has played 2,446 games, so will pass the 2,500 milestone this season. He has collected 2,812 hits, so could pass 3,000 if he plays into 1970. And the next base he steals will be his 300th. How many sluggers ever did that?

One bets that Willie Mays, two-time MVP, four-time home-run champion, four-time stolen-base champion and one-time batting champion, has to be a cinch for the Hall of Fame, certainly and swiftly, when he quits playing.

If he quits playing. For there he is still, walking alone into the Giant dressing room, kidding with a kid, pulling on those old familiar flannels number 24, clattering down the ramp, sitting quietly in a corner of the dugout, talking softly with a young outfielder, picking up a bat and going up to take a few practice cuts, then taking up a glove and running out to center field with the arc lights making day out of night and the murmur of the crowd rising expectantly with the coming of another game. Hasn't he always been there? When won't he be there?

BILL LIBBY is a frequent contributor to national magazines—and a West Coast Willie-watcher of long standing. He lives in Los Angeles.

WILLIE MAYS

Year	Club	Lea	Pos	AB	R	H	HR	RBI	Avg
1950	Trenton _____	Inter-St.	OF	306	50	108	4	55	.353
1951	Minneapolis _____	A. A.	OF	149	38	71	8	30	.477
1951	New York _____	N. L.	OF	464	59	127	20	68	.274
1952	New York _____	N. L.	OF	127	17	30	4	23	.236
1952-53	New York _____	N. L.		(In U. S. Army)					
1954	New York _____	N. L.	OF	565	119	195	41	110	.345
1955	New York _____	N. L.	OF	580	123	185	51	127	.319
1956	New York _____	N. L.	OF	578	101	171	36	84	.296
1957	New York _____	N. L.	OF	585	112	195	35	97	.333
1958	San Francisco _____	N. L.	OF	600	121	208	29	96	.347
1959	San Francisco _____	N. L.	OF	575	125	180	34	104	.313
1960	San Francisco _____	N. L.	OF	595	107	190	29	103	.319
1961	San Francisco _____	N. L.	OF	572	129	176	40	123	.308
1962	San Francisco _____	N. L.	OF	621	130	189	49	141	.304
1963	San Francisco _____	N. L.	OF-SS	596	115	187	38	103	.314
1964	San Francisco _____	N. L.	OF-1B-3B-SS	578	121	171	47	111	.296
1965	San Francisco _____	N. L.	OF	558	118	177	52	112	.317
1966	San Francisco _____	N. L.	OF	552	99	159	37	103	.288
1967	San Francisco _____	N. L.	OF	486	83	128	22	70	.263
1968	San Francisco _____	N. L.	OF-1B	498	84	144	23	79	.289
World Series									
1951	New York _____	N. L.	OF	22	1	4	0	1	.182
1954	New York _____	N. L.	OF	14	4	4	0	3	.286
1962	San Francisco _____	N. L.	OF	28	3	7	0	1	.250

MICKEY MANTLE

Keeper of the Flame

by ROBERT G. DEINDORFER

As Yankee strongboy Mickey Charles Mantle plays out
the last long summer of a bittersweet career, the sentimental fan—you, me, most of us, really—can hardly be
blamed for pausing to reflect on how very different it used
to be.

Even now it is easy to see him in that other far-off
time, lighted with sunshine in a world more quiet and
simple. He is in Yankee Stadium, an appropriate arena,
noble and murmurous with history. In our memories he is
an epic figure, forever swift and young, pumping an end-
less succession of baseballs completely out of sight.

The particular season none of us can ever forget, 1956,
when Mantle batted a prodigious .353 and hit 53 home
runs, is only a part of it. More often than not, his
thunderous bat carried his beloved New York Yankees
not only to pennants but also into the misty folklore of a
lovely, leisurely game America still enjoys beyond any
other.

If those same sentimental fans experience a flutter of
anguish each time the Mickey Mantle of 1969 goes half-
hobbling up the line in a doomed attempt to beat out a
scratch bouncer to the infield, well, why shouldn't they?
Memories, rich old memories, fade some, but they never
really grow cold.

Back on those glorious afternoons of ten and fifteen
years ago nobody, least of all Mantle himself, could possibly foresee a twilight quite like this. At the age of 37, in
his 19th big league season, battered and bruised, both

worn, post-surgical legs bandaged from ankle to thigh, his reflexes no longer quick enough to track the flight of a live fast ball, caught between cross currents of jubilation that he remains a part of the game and despair that his great gifts are now almost no more, the laconic slugger from the lead country of Oklahoma amounts to a creaky national monument—nothing more.

Not even baseball's version of the Judgment Book holds out a lingering hope for anything better. The final figures for the 1968 season show Mantle for exactly what he is today, a .237 hitter with a full season harvest of only 18 home runs, a shackled giant switched from the wide-open spaces of center field to the rocking chair comfort of first base, a memory who probably ought not be playing at all. In occasional periods of searing candor, Mantle has admitted as much to close friends on the team.

Oh, echoes of those roaring old days will still erupt every so often. Mantle still has some truly eventful afternoons—and, for a while at least, older men can warm themselves on fresh hope. On Memorial Day last year, for example, batting both right and left-handed, he hit the jackpot, the perfect day, five hits in five times at bat, two line singles, a double, two booming home runs. Such days are infrequent now, of course, and they will become rarer still as the heat and travel of the 1969 summer take their toll. But the eternal promise that Mantle might possibly break loose again gives each game an extra edge of excitement for the fans.

"It isn't that Mantle is a bad ballplayer," says fortyish Jack Denton, a west coast T.V. personality who has had a grandstand seat since the Chicago Cubs of 1935 ran off a winning streak of 21 games. "He isn't. He's a perfectly adequate first baseman and perfectly adequate hitter too, I suppose. But things don't really seem the same."

At .237, Mantle's perfectly adequate 1968 batting average ranked fifth on a Yankee team which, while considerably improved over the two previous seasons, was improved not so much because of any Yankee thunder at the plate but because of surprisingly good young pitching and defensive play. On the basis of that fifth-place finish, not to mention the return of infielder Bobby Murcer from the armed services and several other youngsters just beginning to ripen, the Yankees may move up, up, up.

As the front office realizes, Mickey Mantle will help get the franchise moving again in ways of his own. He remains an inspiration to teammates and has become an expert at diagnosing a bad hitch in some young hitter's swing. But mostly he is a totem, a brand name, available to be packed around the league to jack up attendance figures, which aren't all that good, flown to All-Star competitions for a ritual late-inning pinch-hitting appearance, generally a strikeout, stretching a number of meaningless records, such as most games ever played in a Yankee uniform.

The All-Star game last year is a particular case in point. Mantle's performance through the first half of the season no more entitled him to a place on the squad than any other hitter down in the lower two-hundreds—and, goodness knows, the big leagues had too many of them. As the most popular, most hailed ornament in the sport, however, Mantle is a part of the pageantry. After all, it wouldn't have seemed like a genuine All-Star game without the slugger whose bat quite legitimately won him a starting spot so many times in the past. Every once in a while, if only for the sake of novelty, the cynical hardheads who run baseball commit an act of wisdom, which they did last July by naming Mantle to the squad.

Late in the game in Houston's Astrodome, with the National League trying to preserve a precarious 1-0 lead, what has come to be an annual event as fixed as Groundhog Day unfolded. Out of the dugout stepped Mantle. The public address system dramatically announced the name of the pinch-hitter, a touching, baying turbulent roar arose from the sellout crowd and then the familiar, bull-necked figure struck out on three pitches.

Afterwards, the aching slugger let his sagging spirits show in a conversation with several writers. "Last year I flew from Dallas to the All-Star game for just three swings," he told them, his big hands spread out in despair, "and this year I flew from Dallas to the All-Star game in Houston for three more."

Why the aging, hurting player invariably returns for one last summer, feeling as he does, is something only another player would fully understand. Among other things, he loves the life of a big leaguer, crowds, travel, fellowship, excitement and baseball. In the spring of last season, driving through Texas, he felt the blood beginning to pound as he watched a pick-up game outside a school. Like a horseplayer ever chasing rainbows, he constantly looks ahead to that next home run, that next late-inning rally, that next hot streak by a team he has spent his entire career with. And until his Mickey Mantle Country Kitchen franchise business develops fully, he is in no position to cut off what has become a traditional $100,000 salary, not with a wife and four growing sons, he isn't.

For the Yankees, of course, Mantle is worth every dime of that large, executive-type salary. Quite apart from acting as keeper of the flame, he is a dramatic link with the storied Yankee teams of yore, a player who gives a sense of tradition and continuity. A legend already being measured for the Hall of Fame, Mantle amounts to the Most Valuable Player to the men who count tickets, too. At home and on the road, even a replica Mickey Mantle helps spin the turnstiles.

"When we're on the road, I get phone calls in my hotel room from men who want to know if Mickey is playing tonight," manager Ralph Houk says, " 'I want to bring my kid, the man will say.' If I say not tonight, they say 'how about tomorrow then?' "

Just last season kids and adults alike began piling out to American League ball parks in roaring numbers, as Mantle closed in on the last significant standard within his reach. After unloading the 534th home run of his career on August 22, a dramatic countdown commenced. One more homer would move him past the total of the late Jimmy Foxx and into third place on the all-time list, behind—who else?—Babe Ruth and Willie Mays.

Day after day the suspense tightened. Despite a sore right knee, a bad shoulder and an aching hamstring muscle, the Yankee slugger remained in the lineup swinging, swinging, swinging for the eventful blast. And when it came, finally, Mantle felt a taste of ashes—for it was a cheapie, a charity gesture, a blot.

With a safe 6-1 lead and the American League pennant already buttoned up, Detroit's Denny McLain grooved a waist-high medium fastball in the eighth inning on Sept. 19. Blinking hard, Mantle leaned into McLain's act of kindness and drove it into the right-field stands.

While the spectacular Detroit right hander was moved

by the purest of motives, especially with Mantle being one of his own boyhood idols, the attendant controversy simmered for a long while. Sportswriters, fans and television commentators criticized the split-level morality of the McLain fat pitch and Mantle riding it out. Happily, Mantle did hit an ungrooved one—number 536—in a game with Boston the following day.

In a way, the assorted philanthropies heaped on the Yankee star—that cheap breakaway homer, ersatz selection to the All-Star squad, a day or so off any time he wants—have put his career in melancholy perspective, as he rides into the sunset. But he has still provided more genuine thrills than most of us can recall to mind. And it is these things that the fans choose to remember.

Now that his career is, for all practical purposes, over and done with, one wondrous fact ought to be considered. It isn't so much that a superb athlete once regarded as the finest prospect to adorn baseball never managed to breach all the walls expected of him—mot career home runs, most home runs for a season, most runs-batted-in for a season, most, most, most.

The point is that Mickey Charles Mantle, a partially crippled, snake-bit human spirit approaching middle age, actually came so dramatically close to all that.

BOB DEINDORFER, a Mickey admirer from way back, lives in New York City, with his memories of a Midwest youth and a Yankee-of-the-future, Scott Greene, now one. He is a magazine writer and publicist.

MICKEY MANTLE

Year	Club	Lea	Pos	AB	R	H	HR	RBI	Avg
1949	Independence	K. O. M.	SS	323	54	101	7	63	.313
1950	Joplin	W. A.	SS	519	141	199	26	136	.383
1951	Kansas City	A. A.	OF	166	32	60	11	50	.361
1951	New York	A. L.	OF	341	61	91	13	65	.267
1952	New York	A. L.	OF-3B	549	94	171	23	87	.311
1953	New York	A. L.	OF-SS	461	105	136	21	92	.295
1954	New York	A. L.	OF-SS-2B	543	129	163	27	102	.300
1955	New York	A. L.	OF-SS	517	121	158	37	99	.306
1956	New York	A. L.	OF	533	132	188	52	130	.353
1957	New York	A. L.	OF	474	121	173	34	94	.365
1958	New York	A. L.	OF	519	127	158	42	97	.304
1959	New York	A. L.	OF	541	104	154	31	75	.285
1960	New York	A. L.	OF	527	119	145	40	94	.275
1961	New York	A. L.	OF	514	132	163	54	128	.317
1962	New York	A. L.	OF	377	96	121	30	89	.321
1963	New York	A. L.	OF	172	40	54	15	35	.314
1964	New York	A. L.	OF	465	92	141	35	111	.303
1965	New York	A. L.	OF	361	44	92	19	46	.255
1966	New York	A. L.	OF	333	40	96	23	56	.288

1967 New York _____ A. L.	1B	440	63	108	22	55	.245
1968 New York _____ A. L.	1B	435	57	103	18	54	.237
World Series							
1951 New York _____ A. L.	OF	5	1	1	0	0	.200
1952 New York _____ A. L.	OF	29	5	10	2	3	.345
1953 New York _____ A. L.	OF	24	3	5	2	7	.208
1955 New York _____ A. L.	OF	10	1	2	1	1	.200
1956 New York _____ A. L.	OF	24	6	6	3	4	.250
1957 New York _____ A. L.	OF	19	3	5	1	2	.263
1958 New York _____ A. L.	OF	24	4	6	2	3	.250
1960 New York _____ A. L.	OF	25	8	10	3	11	.400
1961 New York _____ A. L.	OF	6	0	1	0	0	.167
1962 New York _____ A. L.	OF	25	2	3	0	5	.120
1963 New York _____ A. L.	OF	15	1	2	1	1	.133
1964 New York _____ A. L.	OF	24	8	8	3	8	.333

JUAN MARICHAL

What's Wrong With Avis?

by JAMES ELLISON

When the 1968 season is recalled by hot-stove enthusiasts, by baseball bores like myself who occasionally must escape from Vietnam and racial crises into the complexities of baseball statistics, the names Bob Gibson and Dennis Dale McLain will dominate the rest. Their exploits, the stuff of which myths are made, are recorded elsewhere in this book—McLain's 31 wins and Gibson's 1.12 ERA, an all-time major-league record for stinginess.

Michael Francis McCormick, a journeyman pitcher, or if you're feeling charitable a minimal star, captured the Cy Young Award for 1967, winning 22 games to top the National League.

And from 1963 through his retirement at the close of the 1966 season, a man by the name of Koufax reigned as king of the pitching world, claiming the Cy Young Award three times in four years. The name Koufax was synonymous with pitching brilliance.

You could say that he was Hertz.

And we all knew who Avis was. . . .

Avis, of course, was Juan Antonio Marichal (pronounced Mahr-ee-CHAHL), a high-kicking, baby-faced Dominican with 13 pitches in his repertoire, every one of which he could pinpoint on a dime—fastball, curve, slider and screwball, thrown side-arm, overhand and three-quarters, with change-ups on the fastball and curve. Marichal-Avis waiting in the wings for Koufax-Hertz to close up shop. . . . And at the dawn of the 1967 season, Avis was ready to take over.

Only it didn't happen. Marichal's lock on that Hertz franchise seemed certain through July, 1967, but on August 4 he pulled a hamstring muscle and worked only 37 innings thereafter. He concluded the season a 14-game winner. And once again writers were writing pieces about him entitled "Juan Marichal at the Crossroads."

So he had to prove himself all over again come 1968, just as he had been forced to do so many times before. And he did—with a vengeance. For a sleepy Giant team full of fading stars scratching to stay at the .500 mark most of the year, Marichal merely worked 326 innings, the most in the league. He merely won 26 games, the most in the league. He merely completed 30 games, not only tops in major-league baseball, but the most in three decades! His ratio of walks to innings pitched was, as always, the lowest in either league.

But the fact still remains—Bob Gibson grabbed the Hertz franchise. Juan was second again. The Cy Young Award eluded him for another year. Not only that, but his critics point out that he has become easier to hit than in days of yore. He surrendered 295 base hits in 1968, a mark of generosity not surpassed since Robin Roberts gave up over 300 thirteen years before.

Juan Marichal at the crossroads. . . . In a career that spans only nine years, he has been there many times. On a cold, windy night in 1960 young Juan entered the big leagues, throwing a one-hitter against the Philadelphia Phillies. Before the season ended he compiled a 6-2 record —and even his freshman year had begun inauspiciously. While trying to pitch his way onto the Giants as a springtime rookie, a line drive cracked him in the groin putting him out of action for two months.

Marichal might have done better than 13-10 in 1961 except for a spiked heel at first base—compliments of Duke Snider—which ended his season in a hurry on September 9. That was the year Alvin Dark instituted a complete-game plan with his pitchers on the theory that they were shirking nine-inning work. As a result, Juan, facing the Pirates, wrenched his weak right ankle early in the game while fielding a grounder. Dark ran out to the mound, drawled "Good luck," and returned to the bench. Marichal went on to pitch a five-hit shutout, but there was little love between the Laguna Verde, Montecristi, Dominican Republic, pitcher and his manager from the dripping cypresses of Louisiana.

Nineteen sixty-two truly set the pattern for Marichal. Greatness not fully realized; a great beginning somehow sullied; brilliance somewhat tarnished.

Juan had just gotten married, the Giants were off to one of their patented fast starts—the future looked bright. On opening day in Candlestick Park, Juan pitched a three-hitter against the Braves, beating them 6-0, striking out ten men. With the Giants chasing the Dodgers toward an ultimate playoff, Marichal, only in his second full season, had become the team's big winner, its stopper. He turned into September with 17 wins and seemed sure to be a twenty-game winner, plus. But again a Dodger spiked him—Willie Davis this time—on a close play at first base. And Marichal, inactive for several weeks, managed only one more victory. Worse, Dark lost his confidence in Marichal, even implying that he was a shirker. In the last game of the Giant-Dodger playoff Marichal was bombed out of the box (though the Giants went on to win the game and the pennant). In the fourth game of the World Series with the Yankees, Marichal hit his hand trying to bunt and put on a vivid display of anger. He was taken out and Dark said, "He won't pitch again in the Series even if it rains for a week." Cy Young Award—Don Drysdale.

Nineteen sixty-three was a great year for Juan. His 25 victories tied Koufax; he struck out 248 men. But Koufax's ERA was an almost invisible 1.88 and besides, the Dodgers won the pennant, with Sandy winning the Cy Young Award, as well as the MVP.

Chalk up another Avis year for Juan Marichal.

In 1964 there was further incident with Dark over his star pitcher's condition. Moving along brilliantly and keeping the Giants close to the Phillies, Juan injured his back and languished for several weeks in a New York hospital. Result—pennant out the window. Cy Young Award out the window. Hertz franchise out the window. A great year, yes—a 21-8 record, a 2.48 ERA, 206 strikeouts—but not the year that would finally make him the number one man.

Like a victim of Greek tragedy, Marichal followed his fate a step further in 1965. By the night of August 22nd, with the Giants again involved in a blistering pennant race, Marichal was (and no ifs, ands or buts this time) outpitching the great Koufax. Juan led Sandy in ERA, in victories and he had already pitched nine shutouts. But that night, pitching against Koufax in what would prove to be their final matchup, Marichal creased John Roseboro's skull with a baseball bat, and when he returned from his suspension the Giants were a confused, deflated team and he was an indifferent pitcher. Many a sports writer stated confidently that Marichal would not survive as a big leaguer, that the incident with Roseboro had made him a psychological cripple.

Cy Young Award—Koufax. Pennant—Dodgers. Juan Marichal—once again at the crossroads. . . .

And as he always has, he bounced back. He was so fabulous in fact that *Time* made him their subject for a cover story on June 10, 1966, by which date he had won 10 straight games and sported an ERA of 0.80, or something between a shutout and one run a game. But again Marichal ran into bad times. His health was below par all season, and he suffered at various times from a stiff neck, a hurting back, a swollen elbow, a sore shoulder. To top off the miseries, he missed two pitching turns when his friend, Manny Mota of the Pirates, slammed a car door on a finger of his right—his pitching—hand. Still, he managed to log 307 innings of pitching; to win 25 games for the second time in his career; to strike out 222 batters and to finish with a 2.23 ERA, his second lowest ever. Koufax, however, was better. In fact Koufax was more brilliant in his final year than he had ever been before.

That ends our history lesson and brings up the question many fans must ask themselves about Juan: Will he finally become number one? Will he ever put all his great gifts together and dominate all other pitchers in a given year? Will he win that Hertz franchise at last? No one, of course, can say, but I will venture a guess. I doubt that he will. A bit of tragedy lurks around Juan, and his luck seems a little like New England weather—open and shut. Sun and blue sky never stay with him for very long at a time.

Over his career, though, a case can be made that he already *is* number one. Better than Gibson is, even better than Koufax was. In only eight years and two months of big-league pitching, with plenty of time out for a thick catalogue of miseries. Marichal has already won 170 games. His won-lost percentage today is the highest ever recorded in the National League. His ERA is one of the lowest ever recorded in the National League. Although not considered a strikeout pitcher, he has 1,635 strikeouts to his credit, or nearly 200 a year, and has walked only 449 batters, or fewer than 50 a year.

All-Star records are not considered of much significance, but Marichal's is too incredible to go without mention. In seven games he has pitched 16 innings, allowing seven hits and one earned run. He has struck out 11 batters and walked only one (the plate umpire may have choked). His ERA is 0.50. He is 2-0.

Whether or not Marichal is the best pitcher in his time (a case can certainly be made that he is) there is no doubt about one thing. He will high-kick his way into the Hall of Fame before he's through.

All right—maybe that Hertz franchise will never be his. So what's wrong with Avis?

JAMES WHITFIELD ELLISON is Editor of Special Books for the Book-of-the-Month Club and a softball pitcher-novelist in his spare hours. He lives in Stamford, Conn., where he listens to radio broadcasts of San Francisco ball games.

JUAN MARICHAL

Year	Club	Lea	IP	W	L	SO	BB	H	ERA
1958	Mich. City	Midwest	245	21	8	246	50	200	1.87
1959	Springfield	Eastern	271	18	13	208	47	238	2.39
1960	Tacoma	P. C.	139	11	5	121	34	116	3.11
1960	San Francisco	N. L.	81	6	2	58	28	59	2.67
1961	San Francisco	N. L.	185	13	10	124	48	183	3.89
1962	San Francisco	N. L.	263	18	11	153	90	233	3.35
1963	San Francisco	N. L.	321	25	8	248	61	259	2.41
1964	San Francisco	N. L.	269	21	8	206	52	241	2.48
1965	San Francisco	N. L.	295	22	13	240	46	224	2.14
1966	San Francisco	N. L.	307	25	6	222	36	228	2.23
1967	San Francisco	N. L.	202	14	10	166	42	195	2.76
1968	San Francisco	N. L.	325	26	9	218	46	295	2.43
World Series									
1962	San Francisco	N. L.	4	0	0	4	2	2	0.00

FRANK HOWARD

Washington's Walloper

by RAY ROBINSON

In a year of The Popup and a debasement of Hitter Power, with proven sluggers like Aaron, Mantle and Clemente becoming the most notable casualties of the general anemia afflicting the game, Washington's Frank Oliver Howard suddenly burst forth in all his six-foot, seven-inch, 260-pound glory as the greatest home-run hitter in baseball.

Howard's new rise to eminence came as a distinct surprise and shock to many, despite his 36 homers of 1967, which put him behind only Boston's Carl Yastrzemski and Minnesota's Harmon Killebrew. His 44 homers in '68; his ten homers in one May week of blasting, breaking a record set by Babe Ruth back in 1930 and tied by Hank Greenberg in 1938; his frequent busting-up of ball games for a wretched team that won fewer contests than any other club in either league, all served to raise many eyebrows.

But there are those who have somehow anticipated this sort of performance from Howard. After all, it wasn't too long ago—on Oct. 2, 1963, to be exact, that Howard, then playing in his first and only World Series as right-fielder for the Los Angeles Dodgers—hit a ball that almost departed the borough of the Bronx. It came in the second inning, off the left-handed delivery of Whitey Ford, a pretty tricky pitcher for years with the Yankees. Mickey Mantle, playing the stadium's deep center field deeper than usual, couldn't have caught up to the ball with a Honda.

By unanimous consent it was the longest two-bagger ever hit in the Yankee Stadium—and maybe any place else.

"That ball would have been up in the 30th row of Chavez Ravine," said Maury Wills, then a teammate of Howard. And others insisted that had Wills himself been running, or perhaps Willie Davis, it would have been the easiest home run-inside-the-park ever negotiated.

However, just a year after that historic blast, Howard's batting average, never too high to begin with, had sunk to a depressing low of .226. His home-run total was down to 24 and the Dodgers decided to unload the big boy, who had cost them $108,000 of bonus money when he emerged from Ohio State in 1958. It was the Senators who decided to take a chance on Howard, who seemed to have given up on the Dodgers almost to the same extent that they had given up on him.

The Dodgers simply felt that Howard, who might have become a great pro basketball player, had never lived up to his potential. Frank, too, seemed so depressed with his unfulfilled career that he had quit the Los Angeles training camp in 1964, complaining that he really wanted to spend more time with his family. When he finally returned to the club, he had an unhappy season. "The next Babe Ruth," Arthur Daley once wrote, "was having trouble in becoming first Frank Howard."

The Senators traded a respected southpaw, Claude Osteen and infielder John Kennedy, to the Dodgers, while Howard was one of five Dodgers transferred to Washington. The best of the lot who joined Howard with the Senators was Ken McMullen, who is still the team's third baseman.

"If I had remained with the Dodgers," Frank Howard said last year, while he was being interviewed in the midst of a hot home-run streak that had all the writers measuring him against Roger Maris' progress in 1961, "I'd be on my way out of baseball now. I was stagnating on the bench. I was a platoon player and not many of these guys stay around ten years."

If it is possible at all to account for "Hondo" (that is the nickname he has carried since his minor-league days in Green Bay and Spokane) Howard's arrival as the home-run hitter he was always cracked up to be, it possibly dates from the day Gil Hodges, his first manager in

Washington, urged him to "relax." This would seem like highly unnecessary advice to give anyone playing for a constant loser like the Senators. But Frank has always been high-strung and intense. He has attempted to understand and rationalize the periodic booing and razzing he has been subjected to from the fans, both in Los Angeles and Washington. But he has been truly hurt by it—this supposedly easy-going, Goliath of a man who has smoldered with resentment against the slings and arrows cast at him by small-minded men paying their way into the ball park to malign him and assuage their own frustrations.

But he tried to follow Hodges' advice, even if it was against his nature: relax, take it easy, don't red-neck when they call you ox or oaf or butcher or overpaid. He relaxed so much in 1965 that his HR output was down to 21 and in 1966 it was lower still, at 18. Here, with a team that was rarely in the pennant race after opening day, Howard had little pressure on his broad shoulders. Yet, the big, loose, free swing wasn't producing homers, wasn't batting in the runs that the Senators needed to move away from the second division.

Hodges, in some ways the same strong-willed, devoted scoutmaster type that his disciple is, called Howard in again.

"You should be hitting a lot more homers," Gil began. "I think you might try spreading out your stance. That might help you get the ball in the air more." The same suggestion had been put to Frank in his last year with the Dodgers. The advice-giver had been Leo Durocher, then Walter Alston's noisy coach aide. But Frank hadn't taken kindly to the tip, even if it had come from the mouth of one of baseball's most knowledgable masterminds.

But, now with Gil Hodges talking to him like a kindly uncle, Frank, at last, was more responsive.

"I'll give it a try," said Howard, somewhat fearful as most people are, of trying something new, changing a style or a manner or a technique after years, unbending years, of doing something the same way.

In 1967 Howard experimented with Hodges' suggestion. Although he got off to a slow start, one that might have discouraged a lesser man, the balls soon began jumping off his long bat. Line drives found outfield walls and beyond.

There was the constant tape-measure talk and the usual hyperbole about "busting up seats" and "killing people" walking outside the park with long fly balls. At All-Star time in '67 he had 24 HRs. He finished the year with 36, his highest mark since the 31 he'd hit in 1962 in Los Angeles. He might have gone higher if he hadn't been troubled during the season with a leg injury.

In 1968 Gil Hodges was gone from Washington. His skill at handling men had won him the job of manager with New York's Mets. Now it was Jim Lemon that Howard worked for. Oddly, Lemon is almost as tall as Howard, though his weight only hovers around 210 pounds. In some respects, too, Lemon could be counted on to have a special empathy for Howard's problems, for during his major-league career (mostly with Washington), Lemon had been rated as a lunging, clumsy slugger of the Howard type.

During the winter Lemon chatted on the phone with Howard, who was spending his time in frozen Green Bay, with his home-town wife, Carol, and his three boys and two girls. Frank told Lemon that everyone had been telling him since he broke into baseball just what he was doing wrong but that he'd be willing to try anything that Lemon had to offer.

What Lemon had to offer was the hint that Frank should move in closer to the plate. "You'll get a better look at a breaking pitch," said the manager. "If you move closer those outside pitches will look a lot fatter to you."

So, with his new stance, and a slightly more controlled swing, Howard entered his 11th season of pro baseball, at the age of 31. In little more than a month, the big guy was the most talked-about man in the game.

With 17 homers in the Senator's first 35 games and ten HRs in twenty times at bat over six straight games, Frank was the man with the hot hand. But he tried to keep his performance in some kind of reasonable perspective. "I'm just on a hot streak," he said. "Everybody in this game, except maybe Mays or Kaline, is basically a streak hitter. There's an old saying in this business that water finds its own level. That logic also applies to me. As far as my being a super-star, forget it. I'll be happy to finish up with .275 and 35 homers."

Howard, of course, did far better than that in the HR

department. For, with his collecton of 44, that included some of the longest drives seen in years in the American League (one blast, hit off Detroit's Mickey Lolich, cleared the left-field roof at Tiger Stadium), Howard surpassed anything he'd ever done before in his career. But by finishing with an average of .274 he came within a point of his prediction. His 106 runs batted in, second only to Ken Harrelson's league-leading 109, was his top amount in the majors, since his 119 of 1962.

Outside experts, called in to analyze the Howard phenomenon, were sometimes brutally frank. For instance, Joe Medwick, a Hall-of-Famer, with a lifetime average of .324, suggested that Frank "has been hammering at the door for a long time as a good hitter. Possibly he's adjusted to the way pitchers work him. He had a good stroke for a while. Then he might go 0-for-25. A groove like that goes as fast as it comes."

When asked for an explanation of his home-run improvement, Howard was equally frank. "I'm not kidding myself into thinking I'm somebody else," he said. "I may be hitting the ball better than any time in my life because I'm standing closer to the plate and seeing the ball better. And I'm trying to swing at anything that's close enough to get contact—and I've been getting contact. But nothing else is really different. I'm still not consistent. I'm still the same man."

However, now going on 32, Frank Howard is a different man than the gawky youngster who reported to the Dodgers over a decade ago. For one, he is now respected for his power, which is a proven talent where once it was only *suggested* that with his size he should hit 50 homers every year. For another thing, he is decidedly happier with his lot in life ("I do the best I can") with a club that seems to be grateful for whatever he can do to lift them out of the doldrums. For a third, he makes $55,000 a year, thanks to a $5,000 bonus that Washington General Manager George Selkirk tacked onto his salary immediately after Howard's splurge of May homers last year.

Fourth, Frank Howard is now somebody whom other clubs would like to have on their rosters. During the last World Series rumors were floating around Detroit that the slugger might be traded to Cleveland for a handful of Indians. It didn't happen. But it was a far cry from

Howard's being just one-fifth of a package that brought him to Washington. In 1969 he may even go to first base permanently for the Nats.

Fifth, Frank is now the all-time Senators' home-run champ for a single season, and he has gone from ninth to fifth place on the Senators' all-time HR list. His 44 topped Harmon Killebrew's 42 of 1959 and Roy Sievers' 42 of 1957. And sixth, he made the American League All-Star team last year for the first time—and is proud of it.

Today, the gentle gargantua of the Senators doesn't chase after any false dreams. He doesn't think he'll ever bat .300—and he doesn't think he'll ever race Babe Ruth or Roger Maris down to the wire. But it might—it just might—happen, with lots of that "contact" that Frank talks about and a little bit of luck.

"I know my limitations," he says, "but I'd even take a .260 average if I could hit 61 home runs."

FRANK HOWARD

Year	Club	Lea	Pos	AB	R	H	HR	RBI	Avg
1958	Green Bay	Three-I	OF-P	487	104	162	37	119	.333
1958	Los Angeles	N. L.	OF	29	3	7	1	2	.241
1959	Victoria	Texas	OF-3B	261	59	93	27	79	.356
1959	Los Angeles	N. L.	OF	21	2	3	1	6	.143
1959	Spokane	P. C.	OF-1B	295	43	94	16	47	.319
1960	Spokane	P. C.	1B	97	17	36	4	24	.371
1960	Los Angeles	N. L.	OF-1B	448	54	120	23	77	.268
1961	Los Angeles	N. L.	OF-1B	267	36	79	15	45	.296
1962	Los Angeles	N. L.	OF	493	80	146	31	119	.296
1963	Los Angeles	N. L.	OF	417	58	114	28	64	.273
1964	Los Angeles	N. L.	OF	433	60	98	24	69	.226
1965	Washington	A. L.	OF	516	53	149	21	84	.289
1966	Washington	A. L.	OF	493	52	137	18	71	.278
1967	Washington	A. L.	OF-1B	519	71	133	36	89	.256
1968	Washington	A. L.	OF	598	79	164	44	106	.274
World Series									
1963	Los Angeles	N. L.	OF	10	2	3	1	1	.300

CARL YASTRZEMSKI

Super-Hero—A Year Later

by AL HIRSHBERG

Although he won the American League batting championship for the second straight year, Carl Yastrzemski did not have an outstanding season in 1968. The Boston Red Sox super-hero of 1967 struggled through a campaign which found him tired much of the time and crippled by a nagging wrist injury for over six weeks.

Yastrzemski, who won his first batting crown in 1963 and now has three to his credit, barely made it over .300 in topping the league. His actual figure was .301, the lowest for a champion in the history of either major league. It eclipsed the record lows of .309 set by George Stirnweiss of the Yankees in 1945, and Elmer Flick of Cleveland, who finished at .306 in 1905.

With nobody else in the American League over .300 and only five in the National, it was a poor year for hitters in general. When the possibility loomed that Yastrzemski might win with a mark under .300, he threw up his hands and said, "If I can't hit .300 I don't want the title!"

For a long time it looked as if he wouldn't hit .290. As a matter of fact, only a tremendous finish, during which he batted over .400 in the last month of the season, managed to put him over .300. He dipped in other offensive departments of the game, too, since his 23 homers and 74 runs batted in were far below his 1967 production, when he won the triple crown.

The man who couldn't do anything wrong in a year when the Red Sox won an astounding pennant had a long, rough summer last season. In 1967, when he led the Red Sox to glory, Yaz batted .321, hit 44 homers, had 121 runs batted in, and made it all look easy.

While the Red Sox' fourth place finish in 1968 seemed a reflection of Yastrzemski's failure to match his marvelous performance of the year before, it really wasn't. The club had to get along most of the season without pitcher Jim Lonborg, all of it without Tony Conigliaro and virtually without the services of George Scott, whose dismal slump never ended. Lonborg was knocked out of action by a winter ski mishap and Conigliaro, hit in the face by a pitch in August of 1967, suffered an eye injury from which he never recovered.

So, even if Yaz had done as well last year as the year before, he couldn't have pulled the Red Sox up more than a notch or two. He was, in fact, lucky to lead the league in batting. A hitter of less class wouldn't have come close to .300 under the conditions.

The trouble may have been too much off-season activity. Yastrzemski was so clearly the hero of the 1967 season that the demands for his services in the winter that followed were enormous. He crisscrossed the nation like an airline pilot from October to February, speaking, signing autographs, accepting awards, and doing everything but getting ready for the season to come.

One of the reasons for his great year had been a set of exercises prescribed by Gene Berde, a physical fitness therapist at the Colonial Inn near Yastrzemski's home in Lynnfield, Massachusetts. In the winter preceding the 1967 season, Yaz worked faithfully with Berde, rarely missing a weekday.

But he didn't have time to keep in shape after the 1967 season. Despite all of his resolutions to see Berde at least a couple of times a week and to follow Berde's regimen wherever he was, he let his precious exercises slide, and paid for the lapse later.

He had showed up in perfect shape in the spring of 1967. Last year he appeared at the Winter Haven, Florida, training quarters of the Red Sox weakened by his frenetic winter schedule, a condition from which he didn't really recover until the last month of the season.

He suffered his wrist injury soon after the All-Star game, never mentioning it to anyone outside the immediate Red Sox family. It was during this period when, with his swing badly hampered, he slid below the .280 mark. In Boston, where some observers had insisted Yastrzemski's 1967 feats were all a fluke, eyebrows lifted as they chortled, "I told you so."

But in 1967 Yaz had made more friends than he had ever made before, and they rushed to his defense. He justified their faith in him by pulling out of his lethargy when it counted—near the end of the season.

Actually, he gave every indication that he would be as good as ever when the 1968 season opened. In the first four games of the year he hit three homers—one inside-the-park—and helped the Red Sox off to a good start.

He had another spurt in late June, when he went on a rampage that elevated his batting average into the .350's. He was rolling along so well then that he might have made it big if he hadn't hurt his wrist.

Although so much went wrong with Yastrzemski, a good deal went right, too. He won half a dozen ball games in September with key hits that kept the Red Sox from sinking to the bottom of the first division. And he hit occasional home runs in clutches when they counted.

One thing that did not suffer from his weariness was his fielding. Just as he has been almost since his rookie season of 1961, Yastrzemski was the best left fielder in his league. No one—not even Ted Williams, his illustrious predecessor—could play Boston's tricky left field as well as Yaz. Fenway Park, with its short fence, requires a master in left, and in Yaz the Red Sox have one.

His arm was as great as ever, his judgment as sure and, as always, he was one of the fastest men on the Red Sox club. He played in the 1968 All-Star game and was named baseball's best left fielder on all the wire-service teams when the season ended.

Those who have watched Yastrzemski's career from the outset still see greatness ahead for him. His big year was no fluke, and the comparatively modest year that followed was no criterion.

Yastrzemski's problems were the problems of every great ballplayer who captures the imagination of the public. He was simply in too much demand during the winter between 1967 and 1968. And he found it almost impossible to say no. So he did too much and traveled too far and got too tired.

When he realized the problem—and it didn't take him long—he knew what he would have to do to come back to his peak of efficiency. He spent the past winter doing it. Keeping his nose to the grindstone and staying close to Boston most of the off-season so that he could work with Gene Berde, Yaz has eagerly looked forward to 1969 as another year of comeback and, perhaps, redemption.

This will mean shooting for home runs as he did in 1967—and probably getting them. Because Yastrzemski has the strength, the class and the ability to prove that he can do it again, he can now be expected to.

He really had nothing to be ashamed of in his 1968 performance. After all, he was the best hitter in the American League and the fourth best hitter in baseball. His home-run production, while not outstanding, was his best except for 1967. Prior to that, he had rarely reached the 20 mark.

"I've got a lot of good years left," he said after the 1968 season ended. "One of them will be 1969. I'm sure of it."

So are a good many others. When a man can lead the league in an off-year, he figures to go a lot further when he gets back into the groove.

AL HIRSHBERG, Boston columnist, and busy author of many books on baseball and other sports, is Yaz's official Boswell. Al's autobiography with "Yaz" is still a favorite in the New England area.

CARL YASTRZEMSKI

Year	Club	Lea	Pos	AB	R	H	HR	RBI	Avg
1959	Raleigh	Carolina	2B-SS	451	87	170	15	100	.377
1960	Minneapolis	A. A.	OF	570	84	193	7	69	.339
1961	Boston	A. L.	OF	583	71	155	11	80	.266
1962	Boston	A. L.	OF	646	99	191	19	94	.296
1963	Boston	A. L.	OF	570	91	183	14	68	.321
1964	Boston	A. L.	OF-3B	567	77	164	15	67	.289
1965	Boston	A. L.	OF	494	78	154	20	72	.312
1966	Boston	A. L.	OF	594	81	165	16	80	.278
1967	Boston	A. L.	OF	579	112	189	44	121	.326
1968	Boston	A. L.	OF	539	90	162	23	74	.301
World Series									
1967	Boston	A. L.	OF	25	4	10	3	5	.400

WILLIE McCOVEY

A Curious Case

by BILL LIBBY

In the year of the pitcher, a few hitters stood out, but one of the biggest of them was hardly noticed at all. Willie Lee McCovey, the 6' 4", 220-pound slugger of the San Francisco Giants, is one of baseball's most curious cases. He is entering his 15th season as a professional, has completed ten full seasons in the major leagues, has compiled an awesome array of batting achievements, and if he disappeared tomorrow, few outside of his team and rival pitchers would notice.

Last season, a year in which hits were worth their weight in season tickets, McCovey not only led the National League in home runs with 36 and runs-batted-in with 105, but he averaged .293, a solid seventh-best in the circuit. And he has been accomplishing similar statistics for a long time now. But the newspapers were not full of stories about him. Magazine editors did not dispatch their best writers to his doorstep. Ed Sullivan did not invite him onto his show, and Las Vegas passed him by.

McCovey is a big man, who swings big and hits big, but whatever the curious chemistry that causes a man to be regarded as a super-star, to reap reams of publicity, to lure fans to the box-office, Willie doesn't seem to have it. With Willie Mays and Juan Marichal, McCovey and the rest of the Giants were a bust at the gate last season. Another in a long series of second-place finishes and competition from the Athletics, newly entrenched in Oakland across the Bay, did not help, of course.

The experts say the Giants lack color, especially with Willie Mays aging away at 38 and slowing down some. Stories discuss the team's need for a colorful star and totally disregard the magnificent McCovey, who is a threat to hit a 500-foot home run every time he steps to the plate. Without anyone making anything of it, he has slowly and steadily established himself as one of the most consistently dangerous batters in a game of declining batting skills.

Possibly McCovey should learn to play the organ, hop a ride on a motorcycle, hit an occasional opponent over the head with a bat, start a romance with a movie star or some such thing. A moody man, sometimes pleasant, sometimes surly, not particularly charming with the writers, never involved in controversy, his image is drab. He does what he does so well at bat, then keeps to himself off the field.

"I'm just trying to do a job I get paid to do," he said late last season. "If I don't get a whole lot of press, I'm not squawking. I'll take it as it comes." A huge man with a long, sad face, large chest, wide shoulders, long arms, large hands and large feet, the veteran, who was 31 in January, hauled himself away from the bench and went out to play a ball game.

Willie was born in Mobile, Alabama. The Giants signed him in 1955 and prepped the Negro youngster in Georgia, North Carolina, Texas and Arizona before bringing him west to San Francisco. At Phoenix in the Pacific Coast League he was tearing the circuit apart with a .372 batting average, 29 homers and 92 RBI's in two thirds of the season before the brass decided he could be held back no longer.

McCovey exploded on the major league scene in the last third of the 1959 campaign. Facing the great Robin Roberts of Philadelphia in his first game, McCovey took four swings and hit two singles and two triples. He hit in 22 straight games, establishing a San Francisco Giant record, before he was blanked. He wound up hitting .354 with 13 homers and 38 RBI's in 52 games and was named the league's "rookie of the year."

Quite possibly too much was expected of McCovey after that and he never quite has been able to live up to it, though he sometimes has come close. When Willie got off to a slow start the following spring, he was sent back to the minors. But in three weeks he bounced back up and has been up ever since.

For awhile the Giants had trouble finding a place for McCovey. He is slow and awkward and something less than stylish in the field. He figured for first base, but the Giants had Orlando Cepeda playing first base. For three seasons, McCovey was used as a pinch-hitter and part-timer. Then for three more seasons, they found places to play him regularly. Both McCovey and Cepeda were tried in the outfield. Neither did well there.

Finally, early in the 1966 season, the Giants decided to keep McCovey and trade the mercurial Cepeda to St. Louis for Ray Sadecki. Cepeda was the league's Most Valuable Player in 1967 and has helped the Cardinals to two pennants. Sadecki has been unsuccessful. It was a bad deal, one of baseball's worst ever. But if it was bad for the Giants, it was good for McCovey, who was freed from pressure.

"Big Stretch," as he is sometimes called, had one bad season, 1964, when he hit only .220 with 18 homers and 54 RBI's. Otherwise he usually has hit .270 or better and three times has surpassed .290, which is excellent for a big-swinging, long-ball hitter. Now, .300 seems just around the corner. His lifetime average is .277.

McCovey has led the league in home runs twice, including his high of 44 in 1963. That year he drove in 102 runs, the only other season he has surpassed the round, fat goal of 100 prior to last season, which was his best ever. He never before had led the league in RBI's.

McCovey now has 268 home runs and with another good season in 1969 can become one of the few men ever to surpass the 300 figure. He already is third high among men who ever wore Giant flannels, in New York or San Francisco, bettered only by two of the best, Willie Mays and Mel Ott.

Although he is considered clumsy, McCovey is a stylist at the plate. He swings hard, but he strokes smooth and invariably draws the rare tribute of a crowd of fellow ballplayers when he is tuning up in pre-game batting practice. Often, when he comes to bat in Candlestick Park, "McCovey's Army" moves into place in right-field home-run territory.

McCovey is a student of hitting. "You hear a lot of talk about natural ability," he says, "but I've found there's no substitute for experience. Hitting is about 90 per cent knowledge. It's knowing the pitchers, knowing what they throw in a certain situation.

"That's why I hate to face a new guy. I have no idea how his ball moves. After you see a new pitcher once or twice, you have an idea what he's throwing. Sometimes it takes a few games against him before you can do anything with him, but sometimes you can catch up with a guy after a couple of times batting against him in one game."

This leads McCovey to an original theory regarding the recent problems of hitters in baseball. He suggests that it is not so much that there are so many good pitchers around, but that there are so many new ones. With expansion, more pitchers are breaking in sooner, he points out: "It used to be you saw the same pitchers year after year and you learned what they were doing," he says. "Now it seems that every time you turn around, you're hitting against some guy you never saw before."

As a slugger, McCovey is super. He has unloaded many extra-long home runs. The one considered his classic was hit in 1962 in San Francisco off one of the great veteran pitchers, Don Drysdale. It has been estimated at 600 feet. Giant broadcaster Russ Hodges says, "Some people say it landed in the right-field bleachers. Others say it landed in the parking lot beyond. Personally, I think he hit it into the Bay."

McCovey's mastery of Drysdale is well-known and has been regarded as unique among pitcher-batter jinxes in baseball history, but it is not now what it once was. Drysdale gets McCovey out sometimes now. Yet when McCovey had been sidelined two weeks with a leg injury and Drysdale showed up in the middle of his 1968 record shutout string to oppose the Giants, manager Herman Franks sent Willie limping up to try his luck. Drysdale stopped McCovey, though one swing almost blew him off the mound.

McCovey holds the record for most 500-foot home runs taken away from a left-handed batter in a single series in Philadelphia—two. The first was propelled to the porch of a nearby home, then erased by a cloudburst which washed out the game. The second was struck to the top of a light-tower, then dropped down and settled on the top of the scoreboard. Since no act of God had intervened this time, the umpire stepped in. "Balls hit onto the scoreboard are ground-rule triples," decided the ump. Mac was sent to third.

McCovey also has had his troubles with umpires. On opening day in spring training one season, the crowd overflowed into the outfield, where it was roped off. McCovey rocked one out of sight. As McCovey came trotting around third and headed home, the ump jumped into his path, waving him down. "I think the ball may have fallen into the crowd in the outfield," the ump said. "I'm calling it a double under today's special ground rules." And Willie was waved back to second.

Still, Willie keeps swinging. Early in his career he was troubled by left-handers who jammed him tight. All pitchers who threw him close, especially high, had some success with him. Pretty soon McCovey was being brushed back and knocked down all the time. However, he gritted his teeth, loosened his stance, hung tough and conquered the fearful problem.

Season before last, McCovey got off to a slow start. At the All-Star break, he had just 12 homers and 35 RBI's. Refreshed by the intermission, Willie unloaded 19 homers and drove home 58 runs over the last half of the campaign.

This past season, though he was troubled by a torn muscle for awhile, he hit steadily through both halves of the campaign

McCovey's cruelty to pitchers has produced many memorable moments. Perhaps the most memorable was in 1967 in the eighth inning of a game at Cincinnati. Gary Nolan, a rookie right-hander, since troubled by a sore arm, but then a sensation, had the Giants shut-out 3-0 and with 15 strikeouts was within reach of the major-league record of 18. McCovey came up with two on and ripped a fast ball out of the park to tie the game and set up a Giant triumph in the ninth. That season the southpaw slugger hit three grand-slammers, too, and all against southpaws.

However, the moment McCovey remembers most is one

Hank Aaron—Atlanta Braves **Ernie Banks—Chicago Cubs**

Lou Brock—St. Louis Cardinals

Roberto Clemente—Pittsburgh Pirates *(UPI)*

Bob Gibson—St. Louis Cardinals

Ken Harrelson—Boston Red Sox

Willie Horton—Detroit Tigers

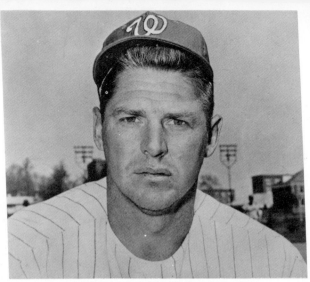

Frank Howard—Washington Senators

Willie McCovey
—San Francisco Giants

Mickey Lolich—Detroit Tigers *(UPI)*

Denny McLain—Detroit Tigers *(UPI)*

Mickey Mantle—New York Yankees

Juan Marichal—San Francisco Giants

Willie Mays—San Francisco Giants

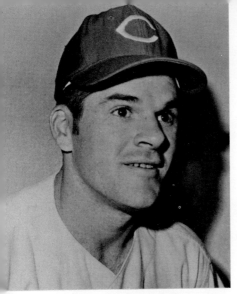

Pete Rose—Cincinnati Reds

Luis Tiant—Cleveland Indians *(UPI)*

Billy Williams—Chicago Cubs

Carl Yastrzemski—Boston Red Sox

of frustration and despair. In the 1962 World Series, Willie came close to the sort of prominence which has eluded him throughout his career. He hit a tremendous homer in a 2-0 second-game win for the Giants against the New York Yankees. The series went to a seventh and decisive game. Ralph Terry had a one-hitter until McCovey tripled in the seventh. Terry still had a one-run lead with two on and two out in the ninth.

In that instant of tense drama, Terry threw the ball and McCovey swung at it. The ball rocketed off his bat on a line toward right center. Even as Giant fans began to scream and the Giant players began to stream out for the victory dance, Yankee second-baseman Bobby Richardson, reacting by reflex, threw up his glove, and when he brought it down the ball was in it and the game and the series and McCovey's magnificent moment were over, all at once.

"I think of it sometimes," he growls now, "but what's the use?" He sits on a table as his huge body is treated by a trainer. "I got a job to do. I do it as best I can. Sometimes it works for you. Sometimes it doesn't. Sometimes you sneak one through, sometimes they take one away from you. Sometimes you hit one a mile. Sometimes you don't hit it at all."

It's all in the timing, you see. Sometimes you do it best when it counts the most and you're a celebrity from then on. And sometimes you do better than most all the time and no one notices you when you pass. Except maybe those closest to you. As McCovey grunts and lumbers out to the field, he passes Willie Mays, who can do no wrong. Mays watches him go, then says, "Without him, we finish out of sight. They don't very often give Most Valuable Player awards to guys whose teams finish second, but there goes the MVP for my money."

WILLIE McCOVEY

Year	Club	Lea	Pos	AB	R	H	HR	RBI	Avg
1955	Sandersville	Ga. St.	1B	410	82	125	19	113	.305
1956	Danville	Carol.	1B	519	119	161	29	89	.310
1957	Dallas	Tex.	1B	395	63	111	11	65	.281
1958	Phoenix	P. C.	1B	527	91	168	14	89	.319
1959	Phoenix	P. C.	1B	349	84	130	29	92	.372
1959	San Francisco	N. L.	1B	192	32	68	13	38	.354
1960	San Francisco	N. L.	1B	260	37	62	13	51	.238
1960	Tacoma	P. C.	1B	63	14	18	3	16	.286
1961	San Francisco	N. L.	1B	328	59	89	18	50	.271

1962 San Francisco	N. L.	OF-1B	229	41	67	20	54	.293
1963 San Francisco	N. L.	OF-1B	564	103	158	44	102	.280
1964 San Francisco	N. L.	OF-1B	364	55	80	18	54	.220
1965 San Francisco	N. L.	1B	540	93	149	39	92	.276
1966 San Francisco	N. L.	1B	502	85	148	36	96	.295
1967 San Francisco	N. L.	1B	456	73	126	31	91	.276
1968 San Francisco	N. L.	1B	523	81	153	36	105	.293

World Series

1962 San Francisco	N. L.	1B-OF	15	2	3	1	1	.200

HANK AARON

A Man's Pride

by AL SILVERMAN

Every year these two guys go head-to-head. The bet is a modest one, based resolutely on the Puritan ethic. The Aaron lover says that Hank will hit more home runs and bat higher than Willie. The Mays lover says no. Last year, as in many years, it was a Vietnamese standoff. Mays hit .289, two points higher than Aaron. But Hank hit 29 home runs, and that beat Willie's 23.

It is a beautiful matchup—Mays vs. Aaron—and a beautiful bet for two middle-aged men to make year after year because it helps preserve the illusion of youth. Just as Aaron and Mays, ageless in their grace, continue to preserve their own youth.

Okay. It's time to admit that the Aaron man is talking here and ... loving every bit of it. It was 1954, Aaron's first year in the majors, when the Aaron man first baited the Mays man, saying, "This kid is gonna be your next big .300 hitter." The Mays man, outrageously smug, shrugged and said, "I doubt it." So Aaron batted .280 that rookie year and Mays batted .345. The following year it was Mays .319 and Aaron .314. And in 1955 it was Mays .296 and Aaron .328, the winner of his first batting title. And the missile gap was bridged.

The years skipped by and both men did everything nature ever intended them to do with a baseball, which *was* everything, and now it is the twilight for both. Aaron is 35 and speaks softly about 1969 maybe being his last year. Mays is three years older and he isn't saying. But

1969 could be his last year, too. Then where will all of us be?

Well, I for one, refuse to concede retirement to Aaron. Looking for encouragement, I leafed again through his recently published autobiography, titled—*Aaron, r.f.* (Right there, that tells you something about the man and about his major problem in life.) And there it was on page 189, "I don't know how long I can play," he writes. "I've said, without giving it a lot of thought, that I'd be satisfied to get in four or five more seasons (well, that's all we expect of you, Henry). When I say that, I want to make certain that I don't get set in my mind to stay around until I wear out my welcome, until the fans look upon me as a welfare case. I want to bow out gracefully, with the other players and with the fans on my side."

You *know* it will be that way with Henry Aaron because he is a man of great dignity. But when the final bow does come, then and only then—much too late—will he receive the recognition that has been lacking all these years.

That's all, really, we have against Willie Mays. He gets the recognition. All his life, playing first in New York and then in San Francisco, the two cosmopolitan centers of the United States, he has gotten the recognition. When fans talk about Hank Aaron, they talk about *Aaron, r.f.* And isn't that a Uriah Heep kind of title for an autobiography of one of baseball's all-time great players. But that's Aaron, and that's why they keep him down on the farm and talk about Willie Mays first, then suggest that Aaron and Roberto Clemente go fight it out for second place.

That's one suggestion that even scratches at Aaron. Two summers ago Clemente was introduced to an Atlanta luncheon as the man who beat out Aaron for the right-field job in the All-Star game. Aaron, who has played in 15 All-Star games in his 15 years in the majors, bristled. "I got more votes than Clemente," he said angrily. "I played left field because Walter Alston asked me to."

The next day Aaron hit two two-run homers and two singles in four at-bats against the Pirates. He also threw out Clemente, when he tried to take third on a hit to right.

'When you're second best," Aaron said afterwards, "you have to try harder."

The suggestion here is that Aaron isn't even second to Willie Mays.

There was a miserable day in mid-July last summer when San Francisco came into Atlanta. Rain fell in the morning and that prompted Giant manager Herman Franks to give his man, Mays, a rest. But Hank Aaron was in his usual place, r.f., and in his usual No. 3 spot in the lineup. That was the only thing usual about the day. Most unusual for Atlanta was the fact that 34,283 people had paid their way in to see a day game. They had come, most of them, to see Hank Aaron, who had 499 major-league career home runs and was now looking for No. 500.

In the bottom of the first inning, Aaron waited in the on-deck circle, studying the Giant left-hander Mike McCormick, and thinking back to his first major-league home run. It came off Vic Raschi, then with the St. Louis Cardinals, on April 23, 1954, his seventh game in the majors. Where did the time go, where did it go?

He stepped in against McCormick and hit a long drive down the left-field line and into the stands, and the ball curled foul by a foot. Then he went out on a routine fly.

Then it rained and the game was stopped. Fifty-six minutes later it resumed, and now it was the bottom of the third inning and two outs, in a scoreless game.

In quick succession, Felipe Alou singled and Felix Millan singled, and Hank Aaron was coming to the plate and the crowd was up and roaring.

Aaron stood in, lean and graceful, in his relaxed batting stance, his feet close together, his bat held high, his sharp eyes ready to receive the message that would produce a whipped snap of his strong wrists. (Rogers Hornsby once said of Aaron, "With those wrists, he can be fooled a little and still hit the cover off the ball.") Aaron thought of the day the year before that McCormick had struck him out three times with fast balls, and he guessed fast ball again.

It was a fine guess. The fast ball came in on him and his elbows and shoulders moved first as he stepped forward with his left foot. As the ball crossed the plate, his hips and torso twisted, his wrists snapped and he connected. There was a t-h-w-a-a-c-k at the impact of ball meeting bat, and it went out in a high screaming arc, flashing through the sky like a giant Roman candle. It went out towards left-center field and the San Francisco center fielder—Ty Cline, not Willie Mays—just looked at it as it disappeared over the fence 400 feet away from home plate.

No. 500, and the crowd was up shouting their admiration for Aaron, and waiting at home plate were not only his teammates but the Braves' president, Bill Bartholomay. Bartholomay is sold on public relations and he had a big trophy with him and as soon as Aaron stepped on the plate and made it official, Bartholomay shook his hand and presented him with his trophy. And when Hank went out to his position in r.f., the players in the Braves' bullpen called him over and they all shook his hands, too.

Oh, yes, that three-run homer was enough. The Braves went on to beat San Francisco, 4-2.

That was recognition, certainly. A trophy, a crowd of 34,000, handshakes from his teammates, and from the president of the ball club, who pays him his $100,000 a year. But it was all rather synthetic, not Willie Mays-type recognition. Aaron remains still a neglected super-star. The flag still dips when the name Willie Mays is invoked, and even Aaron does some dipping.

"Mays is a greater ball player," Aaron says. But at least Aaron has learned to temper his adulation. "He's been a lucky ball player, too," he goes on. "He got to play in New York and San Francisco. They can make celebrities out of a benchwarmer like Phil Linz in New York. I believe if I had played there I would have made $2,000,-000."

The suggestion has been made more than once to Aaron that to get that zippy instant recognition, he ought to open up more, be more dynamic on and off the field. Aaron laughs at this. "I can't change my ways," he says. "I play in my own natural way. I know I'm not flashy; I don't try to be. I have good clothes, and I dress well, but not flashy. I want to be remembered as just plain Hank Aaron."

Then he got to the heart of his own philosophy as a ballplayer. "The way I see it," he said, "my responsibility lies on the field. It doesn't go to speaking out in the newspapers. My record speaks for itself. I can't lead them by any other way than by my actions."

His actions over the last 15 years have been quite enough. His lifetime batting average of .313 is the highest of any active veteran player, including Mays. Last year, at 34, he played in 160 games for the 13th time in his career, which ties Mays for the major-league record. He is tied also with Lou Gehrig for the most years 100 or more runs scored (13) and the most years leading the league in total bases (7).

He has 510 career home runs. Mays has 587, but there is the three-year age gap. When Mays was 34 he had hit 460 home runs. Babe Ruth had hit 470. Aaron had 481.

Mays has 27 more lifetime runs batted in (1,654) than Aaron. Mays has 2,812 lifetime base hits. Aaron has 2,792, 20 less. It is Hank's greatest ambition to become the ninth player in major-league history to get 3,000 hits. Let Mays be tenth.

In the matter of fielding, Mays has always had the edge on Aaron, but it is a soft edge. The edge goes to Willie partly because he plays the more glamorous center-field position, partly because he is such a spectacular fielder and partly, let it be admitted, because he simply holds a few more all-around skills than Aaron (his arm, for instance, is a bit stronger). Matter of degrees, though. "Aaron makes it all look so easy," said his old roommate, Bill Bruton. "When he first joined our team, we would hold our breath every time a fly ball went out in his direction. It was the way he went after the ball, like he was never going to get there. But after we saw him awhile and saw the kind of things he could do, we didn't worry anymore."

You see, there is so little to choose between the two except for flash. And that ain't Hank Aaron's way. "I sit in my living room," he says, "and I always look back and remember where I came from. Life was tough for me as a kid. It made me appreciate what I have today. I appreciate everything that has been given to me. But a lot of people think it's been easy for me. Let me tell you something, it hasn't been."

Of course, it hasn't. He comes from a family of seven, the "middle" child of a large brood born to Estella and Herbert Aaron. He was born on February 5, 1934, in the back country of Alabama and his parents were forebears of slaves. Hank's father moved to Mobile and got a job as a boilermaker's helper at the Alabama Dry Dock and Shipbuilding Company, and that helped keep the family together.

The Aaron family was a close one. He had a happy childhood even though there was just enough money to make ends meet, by a lot of stretching. When he left home at 17 to play pro baseball, the Aarons escorted the boy to the depot and they all cried. "Ma, Pa, Sis, my brothers—they practically carried me to the train station," he says. "I was scared they'd get right on the train and go with me. Ma had fixed me some sandwiches to eat on the ride and all I had with me beside the eats was one little old suitcase. I didn't really expect to last very long with the Clowns."

He didn't. He had been signed by the Indianapolis Clowns, a Negro organization, after he had attracted attention playing sandlot shortstop for the Pritchett Athletics. He also played softball and football at Central High in Mobile, a 145-pound halfback in football. "Once I led the team in scoring touchdowns," he says. "It's been printed that I quit football because it was too rough. That's not true. I got out because my mother had it figured I'd go to college at Florida A&M, and I didn't want to go to school. I wanted to get into pro sports and knew baseball was my only chance. I had to concentrate on one game or I'd never have made it."

It was just as well. He made it big with the Clowns. He played in only 15 games and hit for a .463 average and the major-league scouts flocked around. The Giants offered him $250 a month with a Class-A contract (and wouldn't have that been a team—Mays and Aaron *together*). But the Braves wanted him more. They wanted him so badly that they offered $350. He took it and that was the beginning.

The ending? Well, he has survived 15 years with honor and he hopes he can survive a few more. Teammate Felipe Alou believes Hank, because of his great physical condition, can play until he is 45. Aaron doubts that but he does know he would like to stay in baseball when his career is over. Manage? Of course he'd want to manage in the majors. He thinks the time is coming soon when the doors will be open to a Negro manager. His brother-in-law today works in the Braves front office. That gives Hank encouragement.

Meanwhile, he has accustomed himself to the south again, though he hated to leave Milwaukee. He lives in a ten-room home in a fashionable suburb of southwest Atlanta, with his wife, Barbara, and his four children, Gail, who is 14, Henry Jr., 12, Larry, 11, and Dorinda, seven. His $100,000 salary has made it easier for him, obviously, and Wilt Browning of the Atlanta *Journal* found out what else it meant to him.

"The money means a lot, of course," Aaron told Browning. "But it's pride. It's a symbol of the category it puts you in, up in a position with other top ball players you know you should be up there with. The Mayses, the Mantles, the players like that. But my record speaks for itself. It's not like something somebody's given me."

His record does speak for itself and he does belong up there with the Mantles and the Mayses. Please don't argue otherwise.

AL SILVERMAN is Editor of Sport Magazine and the Santa Claus of the sportswriting fraternity. Each year he gives away a sports car to the hero of the World Series.

HANK AARON

Year	Club	Lea	Pos	AB	R	H	HR	RBI	Avg
1952	Eau Claire	Northern	SS	345	79	116	9	61	.336
1953	Jacksonville	So. Atl.	2B	574	115	208	22	125	.362
1954	Milwaukee	N. L.	OF	468	58	131	13	69	.280
1955	Milwaukee	N. L.	OF-2B	602	105	189	27	106	.314
1956	Milwaukee	N. L.	OF	609	106	200	26	92	.328
1957	Milwaukee	N. L.	OF	615	118	198	44	132	.322
1958	Milwaukee	N. L.	OF	601	109	196	30	95	.326
1959	Milwaukee	N. L.	OF-3B	629	116	223	39	123	.355
1960	Milwaukee	N. L.	OF-2B	590	102	172	40	126	.292
1961	Milwaukee	N. L.	OF-3B	603	115	197	34	120	.327
1962	Milwaukee	N. L.	OF-1B	592	127	191	45	128	.323
1963	Milwaukee	N. L.	OF	631	121	201	44	130	.319
1964	Milwaukee	N. L.	OF-2B	570	103	187	24	95	.328
1965	Milwaukee	N. L.	OF	570	109	181	32	89	.318
1966	Atlanta	N. L.	OF-2B	603	117	168	44	127	.279
1967	Atlanta	N. L.	OF-2B	600	113	184	39	109	.307
1968	Atlanta	N. L.	OF	606	84	174	29	86	.287
World Series									
1957	Milwaukee	N. L.	OF	28	5	11	3	7	.393
1958	Milwaukee	N. L.	OF	27	3	9	0	2	.333

LUIS TIANT

"You Got to Be Luckee"

by RAY ROBINSON

Luis Clemente Tiant, who has more slick pitches than a snake-oil salesman, was spinning, whirling and twisting his way to a fifth straight shutout last May 17, when Baltimore's Boog Powell zeroed in on him for a long right-field home run.

The three-run shot ended a string of 41⅓ scoreless innings of pitching for Tiant, who, after blanking the Senators, Twins, Yanks and Orioles in swift succession, was aiming to break the mark of five consecutive whitewashings established way back in 1904 by Doc White of the Chicago White Sox.

The fact that a blown double play at second base, with Chico Salmon playing the culprit, had preceded Boog's wallop, didn't cause Luis Tiant to lose his philosophical cool. He has always had a private theory that if he is "luckee" he'll kill 'em and if he isn't "luckee," they'll kill him. On this occasion, as far as Tiant was concerned, his luck simply had run out.

"Okay," he said later, with an expressive shrug of his wide shoulders, "so I lose the shutout. I tried my best. I can do no more than that. You got to be luckee to pitch shutouts . . . and you got to be luckee to win."

Last year Luis Tiant, the best pitcher to come out of Cuba since Fidel Castro gave up baseball for non-stop speaking, combined a good deal of talent with a share of good luck to wind up with 21 wins, 9 losses and the best American League earned run average (1.60) since a quiet farmer from Kansas named Walter Johnson turned in a 1.49 mark in 1919.

Tiant did not get the headline attention that other pitchers like Bob Gibson, Denny McLain and Juan Marichal received in 1968. But he has plenty of non-paid, unofficial press agents in his corner, who insist he may be every bit as good as his more publicized rivals. During the last World Series, for example, Jim Northrup, the Detroit swatter, who has become unusually proficient in the art of unloading home runs with the bases loaded, had an opportunity to gaze at Bob Gibson's assortment of blazing pitches.

"I don't think Gibson is faster than Tiant," he said, with conviction.

After Luis beat the Yankees on Sept. 25 for his last—and 21st—victory of the year, Manager Ralph Houk of the Yanks expressed his unqualified amazement at Luis' artistry. (Tiant had won all four of his starts against the Yanks, three via the shutout route and had yielded just two runs on 14 hits.) "When Tiant can fire that fastball from his spinning motion," said Houk, "he is unbelievable."

Mickey Mantle, whose first inning single was the only hit the Yanks managed to earn off Tiant all day, admitted that Tiant's unorthodoxy was enough to unnerve an eye surgeon.

"He's the toughest pitcher in the league to follow," said the great Yankee slugger. "You think he's throwing from one direction and all of a sudden he's throwing from another."

Whitey Ford, who was a pretty cute slinger himself for the Yankees before he retired to the coaching lines, couldn't get over Luis's head-and-shoulder moves, which he insisted was nothing but a means of deceiving batters. "All that stuff comes *before* he throws the ball," said Whitey.

Back in 1964, when Luis reported to the Indians after a sensational 15-1 record with Portland in the Pacific Coast League in less than half a season, he made his first start against a Yankee team that was on the road to winning its last American League flag. Birdie Tebbetts, then managing the Tribe, was quite eager to see just what it was that contributed to such a record of proficiency. Luis never had even seen the cavernous Yankee stadium before; he had about as much familiarity with the Yankee lineup as a man from outer space. But he proceeded to baffle the New Yorkers, beating them, 3-0, striking out 11 men (one short of the record for first-start rookies) and giving up only four hits.

Tony Kubek, now a TV announcer, was the Yankee shortstop that day and he has a vivid recollection of Luis' sorcery. "We were really amazed by him," Tony recently told Thomas Fitzpatrick of *Sport* Magazine. "He had so many trick deliveries and motions that we never really found out where the ball was. Maybe that's one of his big secrets. He gets the batter watching his body motions and then the batter loses the ball. When you see it, it's too late."

In pitching his way to nine shutouts in 1968 and the lowest earned run average in Cleveland history (Stanley Coveleskie notched 1.82 in 1917), Tiant also contributed mightily to the Indians' third-place finish. He was the strong right arm of a surprisingly effective pitching staff that Manager Al Dark put together, even overshadowing his teammate, Sam McDowell, whose 283 strikeouts topped all pitchers in both leagues. With all of his whiffings, Sam was barely able to finish over .500, with a 15-14 record. The primary difference between the two men was that Luis had far better control, yielding only 73 walks in 258 innings, while McDowell gave up 109 passes in 269 innings. Sam also was touched for 180 hits, Luis for only 152.

In his first four years with Cleveland Luis always managed to win more games than he lost (with the exception of 1965, when he broke even at 11-11). But the notion had spread around the league that he was not too durable and that hot weather hurt his strength, as well as his morale. This was an odd state of affairs, especially considering that he spent his growing-up years in Cuba, where polar bears are generally uncomfortable.

Tiant was also supposed to be rather charitable with "fat pitches," a practice that often leads to late-inning disaster. Some also suspected that he devoted too much time to pre-game frivolity in the Indian clubhouse and that he was not serious enough about his career. Regardless of the truth or falsity of any of these stories.

Tiant seemed to be more determined about his career as the 1968 season got under way.

He ran and jogged a good deal to keep his weight down and his wind up during spring training in Arizona. Throughout the season he haunted the outfield on those days when Al Dark wasn't going to use him.

This technique for improving his endurance apparently paid off, for there were times in 1968 that he seemed sharper at the end of games than at the beginning. When he went ten innings to beat Minnesota on July 3, in a truly brilliant 1-0 effort, Luis had 16 strikeouts going into the tenth inning. Rich Reese hit a two-bagger for the Twins to open the tenth and when Frank Quilici's sacrifice bunt was misplayed, the Twins had men on first and third against Tiant with none out. It didn't look too promising for the Cuban with the reputation of bogging down in the late going.

But Luis had no intention of feeding the silly rumors. He went to 3-and-1 on catcher Johnny Roseboro, then struck him out, for number 17. Rich Rollins then came up as a pinch swinger and went down on four pitches, for number 18.

Reaching back for all he had, Luis fanned Jim Merritt on three pitches, giving him 19 for the game. Added to the 13 whiffs in his previous start, this gave Luis 32 Ks, enough to enable him to beat Sandy Koufax's two-game mark of 31 set in 1959. With nine strikeouts against Detroit on June 23, before he notched his 32, Luis also tied Koufax' 1959 mark of 41 strikeouts in three straight games.

The 21,000 fans who watched Luis' 19-strikeout job were appreciative enough to cheer their newest hero in town to the echo. "My best game," said Luis. If anyone had run a popularity contest for Cleveland players last year Luis would have won hands down.

Just six days later Luis was nominated to start the All-Star Game for the American League by Boston's Dick Williams in Houston's jammed Astrodome. It was, perhaps, one of the few negative moments for Luis during the whole season—but it was only Willie Mays, the pace-setter for the National League in so many All-Star classics, who stood between Tiant and two scoreless innings.

Willie led off the game by banging a single past third

base. A few minutes later Willie rode home from third on a double play. That was the only run of the afternoon. The Nationals had won again, for their sixth straight All-Star decision and Tiant was the losing pitcher. After his rough start, Luis fanned two in his two innings of work.

Tiant's mound technique, which is a combination of Satchel Paige's famed "hesitation pitch," and Juan Marichal's repertoire of fakery and flummery, can be positively hypnotizing. Luis himself admits that the whole thing is designed to distract batters—and he seems to have succeeded admirably. "One minute he seems to be looking up at the moon," grumbled one enemy batter, after a session of futility against Luis, "and all of a sudden the pitch is going by you."

"The motion," says Luis, who does everything on the mound but wave at the nice ladies sitting in the box seats, "depends on how I feel and how I think the batter is thinking."

But, according to Joe Azcue, who does a major share of the receiving for Luis, there is more to Tiant's method than just turning his body into a cork screw, or gazing into the center-field bleachers before releasing the ball. Azcue thinks that Luis is a lot more than just excess motion.

"He never quits," says the catcher. "When he's right it doesn't make any difference who the batter is. He'll just blow the bats right out of their hands."

Tiant inherits his pitching talent. And if you would believe Luis, the man from whom he inherited it, his Dad, was a better chucker than he is. "Everybody in Cuba tells me he was better than I am," says Tiant. Luis, Senior, who is still living in Cuba, was a lefty; his son is a righty. Luis, Sr. operated a spitball in the Negro-American League, where he pitched for the New York Cubans. It is highly probable that Luis, Sr. would have made it to the big leagues if he had been pitching today; yesterday, there was the sickness of the color barrier that prevented his entry.

It is also entirely possible that Luis Tiant, at the age of 28 coming into his own as one of the true stars of the American League, will make the Cubans forget that he had a father who could do some fancy things with a baseball.

"I'm just a man with two kids trying to make a living," says Luis.

But if he has two kids, he also has ten deliveries—and that should add up to an awful lot of dollar bills.

LUIS TIANT

Year	Club	Lea	IP	W	L	SO	BB	H	ERA
1959	Mexico	Mexican	184	5	19	98	107	214	5.92
1960	Mexico	Mexican	180	17	7	107	124	194	4.65
1961	Mexico	Mexican	145	12	9	141	106	138	3.78
1962	Jacksonville	Int.	1	0	0	0	1	0	0.00
1962	Charleston	Eastern	139	7	8	99	72	141	3.63
1963	Burlington	Carolina	204	14	9	207	81	151	2.56
1964	Portland	P. C.	137	15	1	154	40	88	2.04
1964	Cleveland	A. L.	127	10	4	105	47	94	2.83
1965	Cleveland	A. L.	196	11	11	152	66	166	3.54
1966	Cleveland	A. L.	155	12	11	145	50	121	2.79
1967	Cleveland	A. L.	214	12	9	219	67	177	2.73
1968	Cleveland	A. L.	258	21	9	263	73	152	1.60

PETE ROSE

He Ran All the Way

by RAY ROBINSON

It is one of the modern maxims of baseball that home-run hitters ride around in Cadillacs, while singles hitters have to settle for scooters. But there is a play-for-keeps guy in Cincinnati—"Cincinnati-born, Cincinnati-bred and when he dies he'll be Cincinnati-dead," columnist Larry Merchant has written—named Peter Edward Rose, who is waging a one-man struggle against this capitalist theory.

Pete Rose missed three weeks of the National League season last year—and the annual All-Star Game—when he fractured his right thumb typically diving for a ball banged out to right field by Paul Popovich of the Los Angeles Dodgers. When Dr. Robert Kerlan, the Dodgers' team doctor, examined Rose's injured digit, he shook his head sadly and predicted Rose would probably miss at least five weeks.

"I'll be back sooner than that," said Pete Rose. He was. Three weeks to the day. And he didn't let such a minor mishap wreck his ambitious plans. For Peter Rose, a combative fellow who does everything but sharpen his spikes before he comes to play, wound up the season with 210 hits, the third time in six years in the major leagues that he has attained the 200-or-more level.

Only one other player in baseball competed with Rose in the hit department last year: Felipe Alou of Atlanta tied Pete at 210. After fourteen years with Pittsburgh Roberto Clemente has gone over 200 hits four times; Hank Aaron is tied with Rose at three, after fifteen years of play; Willie Mays, in seventeen years, has done it just once. Al Kaline, in sixteen, has equalled Mays' performance. And Mickey Mantle, in eighteen summers, has never done it.

Now Pete Rose, who also led the National League in average, with .335 (in a year when the combined average for the two leagues was .236), is out to make a point—a financial point. But it really has more to do with his sense of pride and his attitude about his chosen profession. He wants to be rewarded for his aggressiveness and his driving ambition. He wants to be compensated for all of those singles, for all of those desperate head-long dives for fly balls in the outfield, for those compulsive sprints to first base after he has drawn a base on balls.

"I want to be the first ballplayer," he says, "who is not a 20-game winner or a 30-game winner or a big home-run hitter to make $100,000 a year."

Last year Rose worked—and that is the word when Rose plays the game—for some $57,000. This time out, playing in a small ball park, in a small big-league city, Rose will make around $75,000. If he doesn't get hurt in 1969, and if he plays through a full schedule, he could wind up with a fourth year of 200 hits-or-more, another batting crown, and maybe that 100 grand that he talks about with such zeal.

The real secret behind getting into the 200-hit class is consistency and Pete Rose manages to be consistent from both sides of the plate. He breaks for first base like a man running away from a bill collector—and this type of speed doesn't hurt him in the "leg hit" department. Curt Flood, the Cardinal outfield star, who has made it to the 200 charmed circle twice, says you also "need hot hitting streaks" to qualify. Pete is just that kind of hitter, except he seems to maintain his streak from one end of the schedule to the other.

For example, in 1968, Pete broke from the starting line with a 22-game hitting string, which began with the third game. He had hit in the opener, then left the second game with an injured hand, after two unsuccessful times at the plate. Then in August he put together a 19-game hitting streak, which was finally halted by the Mets' pair, Cal Koonce and Ron Taylor. In 1967 he carved a 25-game binge, which helped him finish with .301. He probably would have made it to the 200-hit class, too, had he not missed 14 games with injuries.

In an era of long-sideburned ballplayers, who threaten to turn baseball into a legion of butlers, the 5' 11", 190-pound Pete Rose sticks to the old-time crewcut. He once told Bill Leggett of *Sports Illustrated* Magazine, why he had not gone the sideburn route. "We've got razors and barbers in Cincinnati," he said, with more than a little challenge in his voice. When the crewcut comes back into style, Pete Rose, the nonconformist who conforms to the old-time belief that baseball is a game that should be played for joy first, dough second, will probably let his hair grow—provided it won't hold up his progress speeding down to first base.

Rose's talents, which are substantially more than just a desire to play the game with the all-outness of a Ty Cobb or a Jackie Robinson, have attracted endorsements from many baseball men. His current manager, the youthful Dave Bristol, who had Pete under his wing originally in the minors at Macon in 1962, couldn't figure whether Rose was for real when he first saw him play. Guys simply don't run to first on walks, don't run out to pick up their gloves, don't run to the dugout for a mouthful of water. But Bristol soon realized the whole show was one hundred per cent authentic Pete Rose. "He was for real, all right," said Bristol. "He wasn't putting me on."

Luman Harris, pilot of the Atlanta Braves, said he thought he spoke for most of the league's managers when he estimated that "everything the Reds win, that hustling son-of-a-gun plays a key role . . . somehow he keeps figuring a way to beat you—with his bat, his speed or his glove . . . he's a most unusual ballplayer."

The crackerjack rookie catcher of the Reds, Johnny Bench, has nothing but high praise for his teammate. "He's just a great ballplayer," says Bench, "and it's just a privilege to watch him—and play with him."

A rival hit-manufacturer, Hank Aaron, has this to say about Pete: "He's got great confidence in himself. He believes there isn't anybody that can get him out." Then Hank points to the yearly goals that Pete sets for himself, almost like a disciple of the Couéism of the twenties. "Every day, in every way, I'm getting better and better," the hoary refrain used to ramble on. And Rose rambles on—and you have to believe Coué made some sense, to guys like Rose, anyway.

When Rose first arrived in the majors in 1963 he faced a certain amount of cynical reaction. His hustle, even in spring training caused raised eyebrows among the veterans, who were startled to find that the then-22-year-old regarded each practice session as a challenge to his reputation. Exhibition games to Rose were more than just a sun-tanning exercise. And all of it would lead up to the regular campaign, which to Pete Rose was the closest thing to war.

When Whitey Ford, the wise-cracking, crafty Yank southpaw, got his first look at Rose in Florida in 1963, he dubbed the youngster "Charlie Hustle," and you get the feeling it wasn't supposed to be flattery. But the Ford nickname has stuck. Rose is darned proud of it today and Ford can be proud that his early powers of observation were totally correct.

In 1963, Rose played 157 games, at second and in the outfield, batted .273 and walked—rather ran—off with National League Rookie of the Year honors. In 1964 he slumped to .269. But from 1965 on he has been the most consistent sticker in a league that has seen some of its most potent batters wither away to the .270s and .280s.

The all-time batting great, Rogers Hornsby, before he died, a few years back, insisted that a man named Jim Rivera was the only ball player in the game he'd pay his way into the ball park to see. Rivera never lived up to Hornsby's endorsement. But there are many today who have picked up the Rajah's tune and Pete Rose is now the lyric. With Willie Mays slowed up just that little bit and Clemente being victimized by too many aches and pains, Lou Brock of the Cards comes closest to competing with Pete in the excitement production department. But an increasing number of the knowledgeable would give the nod to Pete, even over Brock.

Pete comes by his baseballing skills naturally. His Dad, Pete Rose, Sr., was a fine semi-pro halfback for the Cincinnati Bengals and was also a pretty fair guy with his fists, fighting briefly for a living. Pete's brother, Dave, is owned by the Reds and is rated by Pete Senior as the equal of Pete in all respects but competitiveness. But then who could ever come close to Pete for that!

Last year most of the competition Pete had came from a little fellow with broad ears and broader ambitions. Mateo Alou of the Pirates was out to win the National League batting championship for the second straight year. In the early months of the season Peter looked like a cinch for the crown. He was over .400 in May. But then the average started to dip and in the waning days of the season the Pirates' tiny Dominican place-hitter began to give Rose the chase of his life.

Going into the last weekend of the season the Reds had three games to play with the Giants. Rose and Alou, who had to bat against the Cubs, were in an eyeball-to-eyeball confrontation for the batting title.

On Friday night, Sept. 27, Rose played 15 innings against the Giants. But he could reach three Giant pitchers for only one hit in seven at bats. What saved him is that the same afternoon Alou failed to hit in four trips against the Cubs.

Pete's roommate got on him for his lackluster clutch performance. "You're swinging like a girl," said Tommy Helms. That kind of talk makes a man like Pete Rose mad.

The next day Rose got out to Cincinnati's Crosley Field early. He took a half-hour of extra batting practice and then faced right-hander Gaylord Perry in the next-to-last game of the year. The Giants won, 10-4. But that was really beside the point. For Rose let loose with five consecutive base hits against Perry in five-at-bats. It was the type of showing that only a real pro like Rose could produce.

But there was a real pro going up against Pete, too. Matty Alou, believe it or not, went four-for-four in Chicago, as his team was losing to the Cubs!

When Rose heard the news while his own ballgame was in progress, he was incredulous. Imagine, going five-for-five and still being uncertain about the title, with one more game to play.

That night Pete took out his slide ruler and figured that he could get shut out at the plate in his last four times at bat and still pick up his first title, if Matty managed only one hit in four times up.

It was car-giveaway day at Crosley the next afternoon, as Pete's battle against Alou remained the one baseball item that was still important to the crowd of 27,000 that showed up.

The fans made plenty of noise each time Pete came up there swinging. "Everyone in town who knows me must have been there rooting for me," said Pete.

His first time up, against southpaw Ray Sadecki, Pete cracked a two-base hit. He had gone into the game at .335, with Alou at .333. The two-bagger seemed to sew it up for him. It was his sixth straight hit over two games. But in Pete's other two official trips on Sept. 29 he failed to hit.

Meanwhile, in Chicago, Alou was having his troubles— and Rose knew about it, step-by-step. Someone in the park was aware of what was going on in Chicago and the word was passed along to Pete. He didn't have to sweat, either. Matty Alou was finishing the season with 0 for 4 and a .332 average, three points less than Pete.

"There was tremendous pressure on Pete all the way," said Manager Bristol, after the crown went to Rose. "But I've never seen anyone who wanted that title more than Pete."

Now what Peter Rose wants is recognition for the old-fashioned and purposeful way he plays baseball. He wants a quid pro quo for what he gives; he gives plenty and he wants what the home-run hitters and the headline-grabbing pitchers get. $100,000. A cool $100,000.

And don't bet Pete Rose, who has hustled all the way, won't get it—soon.

PETE ROSE

Year	Club	Lea	Pos	AB	R	H	HR	RBI	Avg
1960	Geneva _____	N. Y.-Pa.	2B	321	60	89	1	43	.277
1961	Tampa _____	Fla. St.	2B	484	105	160	2	77	.331
1962	Macon _____	So. Atl.	2B	540	136	178	9	71	.330
1963	Cincinnati _____	N. L.	2B-OF	623	101	170	6	41	.273
1964	Cincinnati _____	N. L.	2B	516	64	139	4	34	.269
1965	Cincinnati _____	N. L.	2B	670	117	209	11	81	.312
1966	Cincinnati _____	N. L.	2B-3B	654	97	205	16	70	.313
1967	Cincinnati _____	N. L.	OF-2B	585	86	176	12	76	.301
1968	Cincinnati _____	N. L.	OF	626	94	210	10	49	.335

MICKEY LOLICH

Improbable Hero

by RAY ROBINSON

As the fall days dwindled down to a precious few before last Election Day and a fatigued and fate-buffeted Hubert Humphrey tried to stem the Nixon tide and diminish the support for a racist demagogue, it became quite clear that baseball's World Series battlefield had given a spiritual lift to the Vice President.

"We're going down to the wire," Mr. Humphrey would insist. "My name is not Mickey Lolich, but I can pitch."

A short few months before the Tigers had accomplished their come-from-behind Series miracle, Mickey Lolich was, if anything, only the third rather unheralded guy on the Tiger pitching staff. He was just a name behind such celebrated figures as the colorful, 30-game-winning Denny McLain and the in-and-outer Earl Wilson.

Suddenly, with three remarkable Series wins under his paunchy belt-line, Mickey Lolich, a 28-year-old, rubber-armed lefty out of Portland, Oregon, had emerged not only as the dominant figure in the post-season competition but also as the inspiration for an embattled politician.

In his own eyes and in the eyes of a goggle-eyed world, Lolich had become an "improbable hero."

"Everybody thought I was an unlikely hero," philosophized Lolich, after the final game of the 1968 World Series. "But I came sneaking through. There's always been someone ahead of me. A hitter like Al Kaline, a pitcher like Denny McLain. It was always somebody else. Never Mickey Lolich. I know I'm not the hero type. But now my day has finally come."

These words of simple wisdom were uttered without any tinge of bitterness. It was a matter-of-fact assertion by a young man who has always been much better than he seems and certainly under-appreciated by those who assign themselves the role of rating the skills of ballplayers.

Events have a habit of changing the perspective of the world—and of fans. Mickey Lolich, who has a refreshingly frank manner, would be the first to remark about this. After all, during the long summer in which Detroit was winning its first American League flag in 23 years (and in which Mickey was contributing his share, with 17 victories against nine losses), there were times when Mickey couldn't get untracked. For his efforts, Mickey heard from his "admirers."

One time, for instance, after a particularly frustrating spell of pitching failure, Lolich was given this advice: "Quit, go to Toledo or run your motorcycle into a wall."

Lolich had no desire to do any of these rather negative things. He had, as a matter of fact, never been in Toledo and Manager Mayo Smith would have been appalled if he had run one of his five Kawasaki motorcycles into anything other than heavy traffic.

However, the testy fan had touched on an issue that has long been a subject of concern to the Detroit front office. It seems that Mickey is one of baseball's most eclectic hobbyists. In addition to his cluster of motorcycles, he has fooled around with skindiving, pistols, singing, drums, archery and slot-car racing. On many afternoons he has ridden his motorcycle to Tiger Stadium, a round-trip distance of some 40 miles, as a sort of preliminary to his pitching turn. Manager Smith admires Mickey's courage. But he remains dubious about the practice, even if on some occasions Mrs. Joyce Lolich, a former airline stewardess, has driven Mickey home to Washington, Michigan, in the family car, with the motorcycle swinging prominently from a specially built rack.

Mickey has insisted that he isn't afraid to drive these things in heavy traffic. He has an expertise in handling these vehicles, he insists, and it goes back to his youth. When he was about two years old, so the story goes, one of these motorcycles fell on him, thus causing some damage to his left arm. To strengthen the arm, Lolich's doctors suggested a series of exercises, one of which was throwing a baseball. Originally a natural righty, Mickey, with newly gained muscles rippling all over his southpaw side, decided to do most of his pointing, writing and pitching with his left hand. Thus was a star born.

"I've got goggles, helmet and gloves," says Mickey about his odd traveling technique.

And all Manager Smith can say, without offending his newest star, is that "It has to be a whole lot scarier driving those things around Detroit than pitching to any hitter."

But Mickey Lolich will not be put off: neither traffic nor enemy sluggers seem to frighten this pleasant freckled-faced fellow.

Prior to the World Series, Michael Stephen Lolich was known, if at all, in baseball circles as a "flakey" kind of fellow who could win a few games and lose some. In the minors, where Mickey started in 1959 with Knoxville in the South Atlantic League when he was 19, he never really had a big year. In 1962 he won ten with Portland. But he also lost nine. In 1963, his first year in the majors with the Tigers, he won five and dropped nine (a frequent final losing figure in his pitching docket, by the way). But in 1964 he went to eighteen and nine and struck out 192 batters. The Tigers immediately developed high hopes for his future.

So what did he do? Very little, really, although his won-lost performance was not as revealing as some of his individual exhibitions. He had a tendency to blow hot and cold. When hot, he was a shutout pitcher. When cold, he was impossible.

In 1967, for example, when he posted a mark of 14-13, as the Tigers dropped the pennant by one game on the last day of the year, he had a 3.04 earned run average, his best ever in the majors. But during that long and difficult year for the Detroits, he racked up ten successive losses. The non-winning streak lasted for 12 weeks in mid-season, enough to make Lolich consider applying for a new profession. However, when he snapped out of it, he did it with elan, for nine of his last ten decisions were victories.

Again last year Lolich was spotty. But when it counted, he was a winner. As the season wound up, he took four of his final five starts. In the last two months he posted ten wins against two losses. He was so sharp at the end that there were some strategists who were all for matching him with St. Louis' Bob Gibson, so that Denny McLain, who was supposed to win everything in sight, could start and win the second game. The idea was to sacrifice Mickey to Gibson, then win with McLain.

But Mayo Smith, who wasn't buying any such desperate scheme, did it the orthodox way and benefitted by it, even if it meant ultimately using Lolich, with only two days' rest, in the final seventh game confrontation with Gibson. At that time, however, he had little choice in the matter, for McLain had redeemed himself slightly with a sixth game victory and thus wasn't available for the clutch game. Lolich, the guy with the flap ears and the belly of a Chicago cop, *was* available. And in case you don't remember, he won.

In many respects Lolich was a truly remarkable performer in the last World Series. After the Cards won the first game, he evened the Series with an 8-1 win in the second game at St. Louis. It wasn't the most memorable pitching victory of all time. But Lolich showed the Cards he was a man to be reckoned with, by hitting a home run, his first in ten years as a ballplayer in any league.

The unlucky victim of the blow was Nelson Briles. He was almost as surprised as Mickey was. In his moment of glory, Mickey trotted to first, forgot to touch the bag and had to go back to make it official.

Then, in game five, with the Cards well out in front, three games to one, Lolich faced the problem of pulling and hauling his team back into contention. In the first inning, hardly before he could get warmed up, Mickey gave up three runs to the Cards. It looked like the curtain was being drawn on the Detroit effort.

But then strange things began to happen. Lou Brock, a constant source of irritation to Detroit, was thrown out at home by Willie Horton when he failed to slide past catcher Bill Freehan. This monumental event, which happened in the fifth inning, helped keep Lolich on the mound. If Brock had scored, the score would have been 4-2, in the Cards' favor. The inning also would have been very much alive—and Lolich would have qualified for instant removal by Manager Smith.

As things turned out, Mickey remained on the scene. In the bottom of the seventh, with the Tigers now trailing by

3-2, every second-guesser in the country was convinced Smith would pull Lolich for a pinch-hitter. Instead, Mickey was allowed to bat by a positively inspired manager—and the unpredictable pitcher dropped a ball into right field for one of the shortest singles on record. But the move had paid off; the Tigers went on to rally for a 5-3 victory.

Thus the stage was set for McLain's sixth game win and the showdown between Lolich and Gibson in the seventh game.

For four innings of the seventh game it looked like Lolich's fine effort was to be frustrated by Gibson's equally effective effort. In a tie ballgame the soothsayers again figured that Gibson, who was as likely to give up a run as McLain was to stop talking, had to win. In the sixth inning when Lou Brock, the eternal base pest, led off with a single, the script appeared on the way to completion. (Mickey had supposedly called Lou a "showboat" earlier in the series. Annoyed by the quote, he called Brock on the phone and assured Lou he hadn't said anything of the kind.)

Everyone in the park expected Brock, in a 0-0 game, to steal. Brock expected to do it, too.

But Mickey had other plans. He had been suckered by the daring Brock in the second game. This time he wasn't going to play the fool. As Lou took a long lead off first—maybe three times Mickey's six-foot height—Lolich whipped the ball to first baseman Norm Cash.

Brock immediately set sail for second. But Cash's good throw to shortstop Mickey Stanley nailed him, as the partisan St. Louis crowd groaned.

With two out, Curt Flood, another classy base-runner, singled. It was obvious he'd try to get into scoring position, too. And Lolich knew it. Flood came off first base. Flood leaned a little towards second. Lolich threw over. Flood was out.

For half a Series Brock and Flood had run the Tigers crazy on the bases. Now, suddenly, Lolich, who looks as much like an athlete as Burl Ives, had snuffed them out. Just like that!

"I can't recall picking off two men in one game before," Mickey said, in a post-mortem, "let alone one inning."

After the pickoffs, the Tigers, helped again by Flood,

who over-ran Jim Northrup's drive in the seventh, finally caught up to Gibson. But nobody was going to catch up with Mickey Lolich.

In the last of the ninth, ahead by 4-0, Mickey got Flood, then Orlando Cepeda, for two outs. Mike Shannon hit one out for a homer. But then Tim McCarver lifted a foul near first base. Freehan glided under it, as Mickey stood close by, lending moral support. Freehan caught it—and a moment later Mickey was on his back, in the traditional piggyback ride reserved for World Series winners.

"I'm just a guy who shows up and gets the job done as well as I know how," said Lolich, the improbable hero of three straight complete game victories.

But he'll never be "just a guy" again.

MICKEY LOLICH

Year	Club	Lea	IP	W	L	SO	BB	H	ERA
1959	Knoxville	So. Atl.	67	3	6	42	53	51	2.55
1959	Durham	Carolina	37	1	2	24	45	27	4.14
1960	Knoxville	So. Atl.	15	0	1	14	20	17	7.63
1960	Durham	Carolina	113	5	10	135	87	111	4.07
1961	Knoxville	So. Atl.	72	3	5	93	76	49	5.10
1961	Durham	Carolina	102	5	5	102	73	92	2.99
1962	Denver	A. A.	12	0	4	10	10	26	16.50
1962	Portland	P. C.	130	10	9	138	57	116	3.95
1963	Syracuse	Int.	22	0	2	21	10	21	2.45
1963	Detroit	A. L.	144	5	9	103	56	145	3.56
1964	Detroit	A. L.	232	18	9	192	64	196	3.26
1965	Detroit	A. L.	244	15	9	226	72	216	3.43
1966	Detroit	A. L.	204	14	14	173	83	204	4.76
1967	Detroit	A. L.	204	14	13	174	56	165	3.04
1968	Detroit	A. L.	220	17	9	197	65	178	3.15
World Series									
1968	Detroit	A. L.	27	3	0	21	6	20	1.67

ROBERTO CLEMENTE

Don't Count Him Out!

by DAVE SOSKIN

That medical phenomenon, Mr. Roberto Clemente, a summer resident of Pittsburgh since 1955 and den-master of a $65,000 Spanish-style, house-clinic in the suburbs of San Juan the rest of the year, is being called by some The Late Mr. Roberto Clemente after the 1968 season.

After all, they say, the man with a lifetime batting average of .314 ended the Season of the Pitcher batting only .291. Plagued by one of the slowest starts in his major-league career, The Late Mr. Roberto Clemente, they point out, scored only 74 runs, was down to 18 home runs, drove in 57 seventh-place Pirates and managed to throw out fewer assorted players of various sizes, shapes and colors from nine other National League teams than in previous years.

Still, is he really The Late Mr. Roberto Clemente?

Many experts call him the best all-around player in baseball today, even though, as Clemente is quick to point out, medical science works daily miracles to nurse him back to health.

In a poll of baseball managers conducted by Joe Falls for *Sport* magazine, eight picked Roberto as the best in baseball. Buzzie Bavasi, formerly of the Dodgers, talking about Roberto says: "When you consider who is the best ballplayer today, you have to consider three things. You've got to consider whether he can run, throw and hit and he must be able to do these things consistently and far above the average. Therefore, the one guy who has all these qualifications is Roberto Clemente."

Running: When he's not coming up lame, straining an instep, pulling a muscle, injuring a tendon or just suffering from plain old tired blood, Mr. Clemente usually manages to do the one thing base-runners are unable to do when he's in the outfield. He takes the extra base.

Although he's stolen only 74 bases in his 14 seasons (and he isn't exceptionally fast), he's the kind of base-runner who's as fast as he has to be. He's smart, aggressive, knows when to stop and when to run.

Throwing: When not suffering from a general weariness of the right arm (which isn't, incidentally, caused by drinking because Clemente neither drinks nor smokes), bone chips in the elbow or pulled muscles, Mr. Clemente has what most people consider the best and most accurate arm in baseball. With a lifetime total of 223 outfield assists Mr. Clemente has ranked first in the league five times since 1955 and second four times. In 1961, the year he hit .351, he had a record 27 outfield assists.

The fact that Clemente can throw is no secret. Many a third-base coach, holding a runner at second on a single to right will attest to that fact. But the way he throws and the way he catches a ball before he throws remains somewhat of a mystery. The ball is caught with what can be called the "low basket catch" and the throw can be classified as "underhand-overhand." These are natural habits acquired playing softball until the age of 17, Mr. Clemente will explain.

Another thing that makes Roberto dangerous as a defensive player is his sneakiness. Often when fielding he gives the impression he's letting up a little or loafing. In a way he is, waiting to set up a runner who thinks he might sneak in an extra 90 feet. Some of his more noted throwing efforts include erasing Harvey Haddix at the plate from approximately 420 feet on one bounce and eliminating the late Walter Bond of the Astros at third base from approximately 40 feet. In the latter instance, Roberto managed to field a bunt at shortstop (how he got to that position no one has been able to figure out) on his stomach and throw at the same time to Gene Alley who was covering third. This was the kind of a play defensive backfield coaches on football teams say you can't teach. Anticipation is instinct.

Joe Brown, general manager of the Pirates and president of Mr. Roberto Clemente's Fan Club, says, without hesitation: "He (Clemente) is the finest defensive outfielder I have ever seen. He is a magnificent fielder and has one of the great throwing arms in the history of baseball."

Hitting: When not suffering from wayward disks, malaria, serious spine fusion, headaches, colds, hitting advice from Harry Walker whose voice still echoes around Forbes Field from the 1967 season or tired blood in the brain, etc., etc., Mr. Clemente is the best hitter in baseball. Even when he is suffering from a chronic ailment.

Since 1955 when Roberto began his career in the major leagues, he has a batting average of .310, even after the .291 in 1968. That's 2,384 hits in 7,635 at bats in 1,953 games in his baseball lifetime.

It would be easy to go on and on about Roberto's hitting feats. A few facts will suffice. In the last nine years he has averaged .326, the best composite batting average in the majors and he has won the batting title four times in the last eight years. Although he's not known as a home-run hitter, he's hit 184 in his career and has managed to hit two tape-measure shots, both over the right center-field wall in Forbes Field, a mere 436 feet away. Enough for statistics.

Looking back on it, 1968 wasn't a great year for Roberto. For most major-league ballplayers, especially in 1968, it would have been a good year, but for Roberto it can be considered only a fair one, especially by the standards he himself has set.

A batting average of .291 can be excused, for one season at least. Roberto actually did suffer from a bad shoulder during spring training. Besides, there were a lot of germs in the air in 1968. It just wasn't a healthy year.

But Mr. Clemente did set a few team records for the 1968 season. He had five hits in a 16-inning game against Philadelphia on July 13th; he led the team in triples with 12; in bases on balls with 51; and in trips to the doctor— daily. Otherwise, if the brilliant base-running, fielding and throwing are overlooked, 1968 can be considered merely fair.

If it was fair for Roberto, it was poor for the Pirates, especially in the standings and won-lost column. This was the year many experts thought the team could take it all and dethrone the Cardinal dynasty in its infancy.

On paper, Pittsburgh looked better than a team that won only 80 games. They batted .252 as a team and out-slugged their opponents, 583 to 532 base hits. The pitching staff, led by Kline and Blass, not Bunning, compiled an ERA of 2.75 compared to a 3.08 ERA by opposing pitchers.

What happened? Jim Bunning had a poor year. So did Clendenon, who had trouble with strikeouts and fans. So did Stargell, Maz, Pagan and Alley.

True, some players didn't perform as well as expected, including Clemente, but more specifically, the Pirates seemed to suffer from something Mr. Clemente, for a change, didn't have. He didn't even take a pill or have an explanation for it.

The Pirates, at least some of them, gave up and lost the most important ingredient needed to win—pride.

Roberto didn't. He's been the team leader since 1966 and he still is. He hates to lose. He plays the game on his own terms and not just for money. He's the highest paid Pirate, but he also has real-estate investments and owns a restaurant-bar near San Juan.

This season he'll be back with aches and pains and pills, maybe even crutches. But remarkably, before the start of most of the 162 games, the medical geniuses, trainers and doctors who work 'round the clock, will manage to have Roberto fit enough to get him into that familiar number 21 and onto the playing field.

From then on, it's an all-out assault, an assault on the rest of the National League, yes, but for Mr. Clemente, another assault on himself.

And in the spring, when the talk turns to baseball, players standing around the batting cage watching Roberto will probably give odds he'll win the National League batting title again. Many players on other teams—scouts, general managers, the regulars in the bleachers around the National League and the boys in the office pools, picking their top players for the year, won't be betting against him.

Even after he finally does retire, when the diseases become more and more mysterious and harder to cure and when Roberto turns to managing, something he hopes to do some day, the chances are most people still won't bet against him.

Only fools will say he's finished or on the way out and dare to call him The Late Mr. Roberto Clemente.

DAVE SOSKIN is an editor, an ex-college third baseman, and a Yankee, Mantle and Clemente fan.

ROBERTO CLEMENTE

Year	Club	Lea	Pos	AB	R	H	HR	RBI	Avg
1954	Montreal	Int.	OF-3B	148	27	38	2	12	.257
1955	Pittsburgh	N. L.	OF	474	48	121	5	47	.255
1956	Pittsburgh	N. L.	OF-2B-3B	543	66	169	7	60	.311
1957	Pittsburgh	N. L.	OF	451	42	114	4	30	.253
1958	Pittsburgh	N. L.	OF	519	69	150	6	50	.289
1959	Pittsburgh	N. L.	OF	432	60	128	4	50	.296
1960	Pittsburgh	N. L.	OF	570	89	179	16	94	.314
1961	Pittsburgh	N. L.	OF	572	100	201	23	89	.351
1962	Pittsburgh	N. L.	OF	538	95	168	10	74	.312
1963	Pittsburgh	N. L.	OF	600	77	192	17	76	.320
1964	Pittsburgh	N. L.	OF	622	95	211	12	87	.339
1965	Pittsburgh	N. L.	OF	589	91	194	10	65	.329
1966	Pittsburgh	N. L.	OF	638	105	202	29	119	.317
1967	Pittsburgh	N. L.	OF	585	103	209	23	110	.357
1968	Pittsburgh	N. L.	OF	502	74	146	18	57	.291
World Series									
1960	Pittsburgh	N. L.	OF	29	1	9	0	3	.310

WILLIE HORTON

Love Power

by RAY ROBINSON

Baseball has its great ironies. Does anybody remember who got the hit that scored Country Slaughter all the way from first base, to give St. Louis a World Series victory in 1946? Does anybody remember who hit the ball that Willie Mays caught over his shoulder, like a desperate pass receiver, in the 1954 World Series against Cleveland? Does anybody recall who hit the ball that poor Hack Wilson misplayed into a home run in the Philadelphia Athletics' incredible ten-run rally against the Chicago Cubs in the 1929 World Series?

Will anybody remember, a year from now, that Willie Horton, who grew up—poor and black—in Detroit's ghetto just a few blocks from Tiger Stadium, made the big play that helped turn the tide of the 1968 World Series to the Tigers? It is highly unlikely that they will, for the 1968 Series was dominated first by pitchers named Bob Gibson and Mickey Lolich, then by a spectacular all-around performer named Lou Brock, then by the hoopla surrounding a cocky, combative man named Denny McLain.

But, in the long run, whether fans remember or ultimately give credit, it was Willie Horton, who battles baseballs and his own belt-line with equal avidity, who stopped Lou Brock dead in his tracks in the fifth inning of the fifth game. The Cards were ahead by three games to one in the Series and they led, 3-2 at the time. Brock, on second with a double, took off like a shot for home when Julian Javier singled to left.

It was Willie Horton who was there in left field to make the play on Javier's single. There is irony there, too, for in an earlier game of the Series Manager Mayo Smith of the Tigers had removed Horton "for defense" in the seventh inning. "I don't think I have to be taken out," grumbled Willie. But Manager Smith said the move gave him his "three best arms in the outfield," and he wasn't including Horton.

Now Horton moved in on Javier's hit (and he doesn't move with the fluidity of Curt Flood or the gliding rhythm of Joe DiMaggio or the confidence of Roberto Clemente) and unleashed a throw to the plate, where catcher Bill Freehan was eagerly waiting for Brock.

The throw was straight, true, but somewhat high. But it came in on the fly and Freehan was there to get it and to slam the ball into Brock's ribs. But, Lou Brock, to his own dismay and to the chagrin of all Card fans, did not slide! He tried to come in standing up, this man who has learned to slide and grope for bases in every conceivable way, and Umpire Doug Harvey threw up his right arm in a signal to the world that Brock was out! Brock argued that he was safe, that his left foot had found home plate. But what ballplayer has ever won such an argument?

If there was a turning point in the 1968 Series, was that it? After all, the Tigers had finally put an end to Brock's base-line chutzpah—and Lolich was able to remain in a game from which he might have been removed. The run would have made the score, 4-2, and the inning would still have been alive.

One can conjecture, speculate and muse. The fact is that Willie Horton had thrown out Lou Brock, a man who has been known to take two bases on an infield hit. But how long will Tiger fans, or any fans, for that matter, remember that it was Willie Horton who stuck his pudgy finger in the dike and saved the Detroits from drowning?

William Wattison Horton is how Willie Horton started his life in Arno, Virginia, 26 years ago. But last summer he went to court to make it just plain Willie Horton. "My regular name is a good one," explained Horton, "but I'd rather be just Willie."

He has been part of the Tiger master plan now for six years and a regular since 1965. Last year, with 36 home runs (and one more in the World Series), he was indispensable to Detroit's surge to a pennant and world championship. A muscular man who reminds baseball people of Brooklyn's great, but ill-fated catcher, Roy Campanella, Willie Horton takes a belligerent, butcher's slice at the ball. When he connects, he hits massive home runs and astonishing triples. It is likely that if he plays long enough, and if injuries (which have continually afflicted him) do not bar his progress, he may one day top Hank Greenberg's top Tiger total of 58 homers. It is more realistic to assume that he will one day beat Norm Cash's 41 or Rocky Colavito's 45.

In the American League in 1968 only one home-run hitter passed him. That was Frank Howard, who bashed 44, in his own sudden display of long-distance regularity.

There were many big moments for Willie Horton last year, aside from his magic moment against Lou Brock. While a nationwide TV audience watched in September, Willie lined the ninth-inning single against Oakland that made Denny McLain a 30-game winner. "I made up my mind to hit that ball and run," said Willie, in the post-game hysteria surrounding the event.

On seven other occasions he broke up ball games with late-inning hits, a Detroit trademark throughout the season. There is little wonder now why rival managers treat Horton with increasing respect and why Bill Rigney, for instance, will admit that some of his California Angel pitchers are "petrified" by the prospect of facing Willie in the clutch.

But it is not only his rivals on the field who have respect for this bulging-muscled man. Willie Horton has earned and won the respect also of Detroit's fans, who waited and hungered 23 years for a pennant. Two summers ago Detroit was a city in crisis, ripped and scarred by interracial hostility. Guns crackled and sputtered in the city's slums and fires burned during the summer heat. But Willie Horton, who stands, hands on hips, in left field, was cheered to the echo by the fans in the lower left-field seats—and many of those fans were white.

Following the grim summer of 1967 Willie visited many ghetto schools in the winter. Always he carried a message of hope: "Work hard, try to stay out of trouble and take care of your bodies."

When an inflamed growth agitated his heel last winter he

went to the hospital to have it removed. He had time to think about his city, its troubles and its discontented black population.

"I thought a lot about where I came from," said Willie. "The people had plenty reason to protest. Every man wants respect and dignity. If you don't get respect out in the world, you don't get it at home." But he lamented the fact that "people took things," making it harder for white people to comprehend and sympathize with the black man's grievances.

During the summer of 1968, as the Tigers marched inexorably to their pennant, Willie Horton used much of his spare time to work with youngsters in Detroit's deprived sections. He is not the most articulate of men. But he knows where he came from and knows where he's going.

The accent is heavy on money and tangible rewards these days in baseball, as it is in almost every other professional sport. But Willie Horton seems to find his own special reward, over and above a respectable salary of close to $50,000, in the joy of playing the game. He does not play with the wrath of Ty Cobb or the ebullience of Mays or the daring of Pete Reiser, who once challenged fences, but Willie Horton stands up there each day, a robust target for pitchers, and comes back for more.

He told *Ebony* Magazine that "I have to hit the dirt in almost every game." But despite the fact that he seems to be the successor to Frank Robinson in this unenviable category, he insists that "guys who don't love the game can't play their best." In a paraphrase of a fighting Leo Durocher statement ("He comes to play"), Detroit's batting coach, Wally Moses, says of Horton: "He come to beat ya, this fella."

Horton believes, as you see, in playing baseball all out, despite injuries and ailments. Last year, as the Tigers sought to wrap up the flag, Horton came down with an acute respiratory infection. He was still in a weakened state as the World Series got under way, but it didn't stop him from hitting a long homer in the second game deep into Busch Stadium's seats in left-center field. It was Detroit's first run of the Series and put Mickey Lolich on the road to victory. He wound up the classic with a .304 average, three runs batted in and six runs scored.

Last July, in a night game against Baltimore, Horton came rumbling in under a short fly ball hit by Brooks Robinson. He failed to make the catch. But, more important, he bruised his abdominal muscles.

Carried from the diamond on a stretcher, Willie looked like a man who would be out of action at least for a week. However, the next day he was right back in Mayo Smith's lineup, guarding left field and batting cleanup. In the seventh inning, as the Tigers put on a rally against the Orioles, Horton went down, when Gene Brabender's pitch creamed him on the arm.

"I haven't been knocked down so often in my life," said Horton. "But I thank God for giving me the reflexes to get out of the way."

Willie might have added that without the reflexes he might have been permanently sidelined a long time ago.

It is a common assumption these days when a club with a mix of blacks and whites comes through to win a championship that something is going right in the relationships between men on the ball club. This is, perhaps, an oversimplification, for it is always possible that skillful bigots can produce game-winning hits that knock in Negroes. The profit motive can still the latent beast and incivility in many men; and so it is in baseball.

But Willie sincerely believes that the Detroit team was a good example of closeness and togetherness. Three of the white players on the club, Mickey Stanley, Bill Freehan and Jim Northrup, are close pals of Willie's. Willie measures the warmth of the ball club with his instinct and says: "Everybody looks like they love each other. That's the reason we're in first place. This team is all friends."

When the Tigers won the seventh game of the World Series last year Horton forced his way through the tumult in the Busch Stadium Detroit dressing room. Bare to the waist, Willie crushed his white-haired manager, Mayo Smith, in an exuberant bear hug and capped the caress with a champagne shampoo. Then Willie kissed Mayo on his bald spot, while the cameras recorded the event for posterity.

The two men have had their quarrels and disagreements—but, as Willie says, there's "love" on this Detroit club.

And a good part of the affection is for Willie Horton, who is strong enough to crush a man's breath out of his body.

WILLIE HORTON

Year	Club	Lea	Pos	AB	R	H	HR	RBI	Avg
1962	Duluth-Superior	Northern	OF	441	68	130	15	72	.295
1963	Syracuse	Int.	OF	78	12	17	2	8	.218
1963	Knoxville	So. Atl.	OF	442	77	147	14	70	.333
1963	Detroit	A. L.	OF	43	6	14	1	4	.326
1964	Detroit	A. L.	OF	80	6	13	1	10	.163
1964	Syracuse	Int.	OF-3B	490	73	141	28	99	.288
1965	Detroit	A. L.	OF-3B	512	69	140	29	104	.273
1966	Detroit	A. L.	OF	526	72	138	27	100	.262
1967	Detroit	A. L.	OF	401	47	110	19	67	.274
1968	Detroit	A. L.	OF	512	68	146	36	85	.285
World Series									
1968	Detroit	A. L.	OF	23	6	7	1	3	.304

ERNIE BANKS
and
BILLY WILLIAMS

Bruin Bombers

by WILLIAM BARRY FURLONG

The sun was still high. It was late season now and the pattern of the season—with Ernie Banks and Billy Williams helping to slug the Cubs into third place—was fixed. It was two hours before game time and Billy Williams was in the batting cage, leveling on the ball with whip-snapping quickness. "Look at the way he cocks his wrists," said a teammate. "He's got wrists right up to his armpits."

Williams would finish the 1968 campaign tied for second in runs-batted-in with 98, just seven behind Willie McCovey of the San Francisco Giants. The man he was tied with was standing leisurely by the batting cage: Ron Santo, a man with the blonde good looks of the Scandinavian and the dark eruptive temperament of the Italian. "Everybody thought this would be Ernie's last year," he was saying. "He showed 'em—it won't be."

Ernie Banks would hit 32 home runs in 1968, third best in the National League. He was 37 years old now—the same age as Willie Mays, the same age as Mickey Mantle. Mays would get 23 home runs in 1968; Mantle would get 18. "And don't think the pitchers are easing up on Ernie," Santo said. "They can't afford to. Ernie's adjusted since last year. He's an intelligent ballplayer—that's what makes him so great."

In the Cub clubhouse, the thermostat waas turned down to 68 degrees. By the end of the day, the temperature would be 73 degrees, because of the heat of summer and the steam of the showers. Ernie Banks, the man they were talking about, sat in front of the grey-metal screens that formed his cubicle. He was sipping a cup of hot soup. Banks sometimes goes ten hours or more without food on the day of a game; the hot soup—taken about an hour before game time—helps him keep up his energy.

"My rhythm and timing has been better this year than any year since 1962," he said. "Not consistently, but often." In 1962 he hit 37 homers and had 104 RBI's. It was a good year but not his best: as recently as 1965 he got 106 RBI's.

How had he adjusted?

"Last year I hit the ball to right field more than I'd ever done before. Learning to do that helped my timing. And the pitching also changed because of that. They began keeping the ball inside to me, pitching me tight. So that enabled me to pull the ball more this year." And that enabled him to hit the ball farther more frequently in 1968. It was only the second time in the last eight years that he had gone over 30 home runs for the season—and he'd done it when slugging was on the decline elsewhere in baseball.

Banks has a practiced extroversion; he fought his way to the big leagues from Negro baseball—he never played a day of minor-league baseball. Williams is a more taciturn type; he made his way to the big leagues through the stern crucible of minor-league play—sometimes playing brilliantly, sometimes not.

As a hitter, Billy Williams was always an artist. He was born with all the natural gifts for hitting but he never built to the zenith on them—as Michelangelo built on his gifts, as Joe DiMaggio built on his. He has always been close to the leaders in the batting race but he's never been the leader. "I've always been second in everything, he said on the weekend in September that he seized the National League lead in RBI's—briefly. "It'd be nice to be first for a change."

He wasn't first this time.

Williams didn't get another run batted in for the last two weeks of the season. McCovey got ten and passed him up to win the RBI total. One reason: Williams very much tended to be a streak hitter last year. In one double-header in August in Atlanta, he got nine runs batted in. In another streak in September, he got five home runs and seven RBI's in two games.

But there is a peace in him, a passiveness that lets him accept what comes in, a perspective vaster than the moment. "When I'm at the plate, I say to myself, 'You've *got* to do it. You've *got* to do it,' " he says. "But if I don't do it, I know the world isn't going to stop. You *know* you're going to have another time at the plate. The minute you start pressing, you're through. You're not giving yourself a chance."

There is no indifference in all this. Billy Williams is one of the best clutch hitters in the game: in 1967, he led the Cubs with a batting average of .419 in the clutch and showed an average of advancing runners in the clutch of .347. So he is at his best when the going is roughest. One reason: he studies the pitchers endlessly. He begins to "bat" mentally when he climbs the dugout steps and settles with one knee on a towel in the on-deck circle. "You get a little better idea of their speed and the way the ball is moving up there than you do from the dugout," he once told me. He also concentrates on what not to watch when he gets to the plate— "the foot, the face, all the things that a pitcher uses to throw you off." Then he begins eliminating—in his growing concentration in the on-deck circle—those distracting elements. "I never watch the pitcher's face. I watch the ball." By the time he's ready to go to bat, he's brought his concentration in on the single element of success—hitting the ball, not watching the twitching toes or lifted eyebrows of the pitcher. He just doesn't try to hit the ball; he attacks it.

He is endowed with one of the classic swings in all of baseball. The swing generates great power, though Williams is not a muscleman—he weighs only about 175-180 pounds and stands 6' 1". But he's mastered the art of transmitting all his power from his biceps through his wrists to the ball. In a gesture as effortless as blinking, he snaps his wrists as he swings at the ball—almost as if he's snapping a whip. He's also mastered the art of swinging down on the ball—instead of up—in order to give it a long ride. "On most high pitches, most hitters swing up at the ball," said one of the Cub catchers some time ago. He was describing the effort to "loft" the ball into the distant grandstand. "But Billy, he swings down on the ball. He uses his arms to show a shallow downward arc, as if he was swinging an ax sidearm and the weight of the head was carrying the swing downward. That way he gets a spin on the ball that keeps the ball going."

To all this, Billy Williams adds consistency: he's always there and always trying. He has now played in 818 consecutive games as an outfielder, setting a record for the run. (The previous record: 694, set by Richie Ashburn.) Along the way, he set a few fielding records—which might be considered even more of a triumph than his hitting. For he is not a natural-born outfielder. In fact, as a youth he wasn't an outfielder at all; he was an infielder. In fact, when he was even *younger* he wasn't even a baseball player; he was a football player.

Williams grew up in Whistler, Alabama, just a few miles up the road from Mobile. His high school didn't have a baseball team but it did have a football team. So Billy went out for football in his senior year and won a first-string role as a defensive end—a *155-pound* defensive end. He played well enough to earn a scholarship to Grambling, but he was distracted by other things.

Among them was the fun of playing semi-pro baseball. He went out for and won a spot as a third baseman on the Mobile Barons. A scout for the Chicago Cubs—in Mobile to scout Tommy Aaron, the brother of Henry—came across Billy. He watched him for a year, and then signed him to a Cub contract. Billy didn't get a bonus; he didn't even know what they were. The only thing he got as a "bonus" was a 15-cent cigar for his father and a bus ticket to Ponca City—the Oklahoma town that had a class D farm in the Cub system.

At the time, he had never played the outfield and he had never played at night. At Ponca City, he did both. "I remember the first ball he ever caught—he wound up flat on his stomach," Don Biebel once told me. Biebel had taken over as manager of Ponca City at the age of 23; later he was to become traveling secretary of the Cubs. He endured Billy's introduction to the outfield. It shortly became clear that Williams did not have a strong arm, that he approached ground balls as warily as a suspicious cat and though he had the speed to catch up to fly balls, he did not often catch them. Biebel went to work to try to help him.

"He was a very shy kid, very quiet," Biebel was to recall later. Billy was only 18 and he was the "extra" man on the ball club. He didn't make the road trips with the club because he lacked experience and skill. "Plus the fact that we traveled in station wagons and there was no room for me," said Billy. At the time, there was a limit of 15 on the active rosters of class D ball clubs. Biebel discovered a way of keeping a player on the roster for five days, then putting him on the inactive list, and then reactivating him a little later. "We were switching several guys around like that," recalls Biebel.

That year, Williams played in only 13 games and came to bat only 17 times. He batted .235. That was in 1956. The next year he played regularly and hit .310. Then he began working his way up—through Burlington, San Antonio, Fort Worth and Houston. He had brief tryouts in the major leagues in 1959 and 1960 but he did not win a permanent spot on the Cubs until 1961. He hit 25 home runs, drove in 86 runs—and was elected Rookie of the Year in the National League.

In a way, that was almost the beginning—not the end—of his development. For he was still shaping and perfecting his hitting style. And he was learning how best to field in the major leagues. He learned how to charge the ground ball and get his body into position so that he'd get maximum momentum into his throw. Since his throwing arm was not spectacularly strong, he learned to compensate for it by getting the ball away more quickly and by throwing with greater accuracy—"I pointed my left foot and left leg right at where I'm going to throw." And then to follow through, so that his right (or throwing) arm and right shoulder were pointed at his target. Most of all, he learned to get the jump on the ball—to watch the strike zone, not the ball as it's pitched. In that way, the outfielder can see the ball the moment it is hit and emerges from the strike zone—and thus get a big jump on where it is going. One result: in his first full year in the minor leagues, he committed 25 errors. By the time he was a mature major-leaguer, he'd cut his yearly total to three and sometimes to four.

That—and the consistency and power of his hitting—has made him one of the most respected outfielders in the league. (He was chosen by manager Red Schoendienst for the National League All-Star team last year.) It has also given him a pre-eminent place among the sluggers in Cub history.

Even more pre-eminent, perhaps, is Ernie Banks. At the time that Billy Williams came to the Cubs, Banks was already a veteran, already a candidate for the Hall of Fame. The reason: he'd helped revolutionize the whole style of slugging in the major leagues.

Ernie grew up in Dallas, Texas. He was the oldest of ten children. His father ran a grocery store and tried to bribe Ernie into playing baseball. "He bought me a $2.98 glove"—that was a lot of money in those days—"and then he'd give me nickels and dimes to play catch with him." Ernie was more interested in other sports: in high school, he was captain of the basketball and football teams (he caught 21 touch-down passes—he *still* has great hands—as an end in his last two years) and on the track team he was a high-jumper and quarter-miler. He never really played much baseball as a child; softball was the game in his neighborhood. But he was good enough at it to be courted by a Negro semi-pro baseball team that barn-stormed in the Southwest and Midwest. His parents wouldn't let him go on tour until after he finished high school. Then he joined the team and began the long dreary trips through the stifling summer nights. "Ten, fifteen, twenty-thousand miles a year and the best payday we ever had was $20—one night in Hastings, Nebraska."

But it was on that tour that James "Cool Papa" Bell spotted him and arranged a tryout for him with the old Kansas City Monarchs of the Negro Baseball league. Banks played shortstop for the Monarchs for one season, went into the Army for two years, and emerged to play another season for the Monarchs. Then the Cubs began to hear of him; in 1953, they assigned nine different scouts to watch him and report on him. By season's end they were satisfied: they bought his contract from the Monarchs, and played him for 10 games at the end of 1953. In 1954—with no minor-league experience—he became the regular shortstop of the Chicago Cubs.

At the time, he was not a burly man: he weighed 169 to 177 pounds—and he plays at very little more weight today. "I carry my weight in my toes," he says with elfin humor. "I've got very muscular toes." But he has wrists and forearms that look like they were forged from tempered steel. And it was this fact—combined with one other—that led to the Era of the Lively Bat.

The other was his selection, late in the 1954 season, of a new bat. He'd done all right for a rookie: he batted .275 and hit 19 home runs. But towards the end of the season, his bat began feeling very heavy—"like I was swinging a telephone pole." One day he picked up a bat normally used by a teammate, Monte Irvin. It was four ounces lighter than his own. "Man, I could really swish that little stick," he told me later on. He decided—in defiance of all baseball tradition—to continue using the bat all through the 1955 season.

The result was that he became the hardest-hitting shortstop in the history of the major leagues. In one six-season span—1955-60—he hit more home runs than any other player in the major leagues. (He hit 248 homers in that period. Mickey Mantle hit 236. Willie Mays hit 214.) Until that day in September, 1954, he'd never hit a grand-slam home run in his life. The next season, he hit five of them—a record which still stands. He became the only player in the history of the voting by the Baseball Writers Association of America to win the Most Valuable Player award of the National League twice in a row—in 1958 and 1959. Not Mays, not Musial, not Koufax, not Jackie Robinson: nobody—*nobody*—else had ever done it.

But more than that, the entire style of slugging began to change. Mickey Mantle, who'd been using bats weighing 34 to 36 ounces, cut down to a 32-ounce bat. Eddie Mathews, at the time one of the great sluggers of the game, opened a season disastrously in 1956 with a 38-ounce bat, then went to a 32-ounce bat in mid-season. He wound up hitting 37 home runs. All the older sluggers of that era began going to trimmer bats: Hank Sauer— one of the great "musclemen" batters of the 1940's and 1950's—abandoned a 42-ounce club for 36- and 38-ounce bats. Gil Hodges, now manager of the New York Mets, cut four or five ounces in the bats he chose to use. It was all a stunning change from the past when sluggers regularly used extremely heavy bats: Babe Ruth used bats as heavy as 48 ounces and bats weighing up to 54 ounces had been known in the major leagues.

The idea introduced by Banks was that a man—a slim

slugger—could drive the ball just as far as the muscle-bound sluggers of the past if he could just swing the bat faster. And with a lighter bat, he *could* swing it much faster. "He's getting 25 to 30 miles an hour more on his swing now," said Lew Fonseca, top movieman of the major leagues after studying films of Banks' swing. Of course, Banks had a particular kind of swing—quick and snappy, instead of the long-looping "free" swing that sluggers had been used to. "He swings like Joe Louis used to punch—short and sweet," said one of his contemporaries of the 1950's, catcher Clyde McCullough. That gave him magnificent control of the bat. Also he had these great forearms and wrists so that he delivered full power at full speed at the very moment of impact. The result: "His hits leap right off the bat—line drives," said one of his managers. "They get past the outfielders before they realize what's happened." He also had great eyes: in a test conducted by Bausch & Lomb of some 300 professional ballplayers of the 1950's, he tested out at 20-10 in visual acuity, the best in the group. That meant he could see at 20 feet what the normal eye could see at ten feet. That also meant he could see the ball more clearly and—because his swing was so fast—*know* he could watch it break or move before he committed himself. "He hits the ball right out of the catcher's mitt," said catcher McCullough.

As time went by, Ernie began having trouble in the field. He hurt his arm one year and to compensate for poor throwing ability he moved in a few steps in the infield. But he didn't have the quickness to grab balls hit sharply to his right. When the arm recovered, he moved back to his deeper position in the infield and, in 1959, set a record for fielding for major-league shortstops. But then he injured and re-injured a leg. No longer did he have the mobility in the field. He had—and has—great hands. Anything he could reach, he could catch. But he couldn't reach as many balls as in the past. And when the difficulties began affecting his hitting, there were some who thought that, now that Banks was in his 30's, he was on the decline.

The Cubs decided to move him away from shortstop. But they didn't know quite how to do it: after all, they were proposing to move the greatest hitting shortstop in the game over to first base. So they went about it in a maladroit fashion. In 1961, after Ernie had played 33 games at shortstop, they moved him to left field. Not first base. Left field. The excuse: his bad knee. But left field was no place for a man with poor legs, poor speed, and a questionable throwing arm. Ernie stayed there for 22 games and committed one error. (In that time, the Cubs moved Billy Williams to right field, where he did so poorly that they finally benched him.) Then the Cubs abruptly moved Banks to first base. (Williams went back to left field—and to rookie-of-the-year honors.) Ernie played seven games at first base—and just as abruptly was moved back to shortstop.

In 1962, the Cubs tried again. They moved Banks over to first base in spring training and kept him there. An amazing thing happened: his hitting began to pick up—he had his best year at the bat in the last ten years—and he turned out to be an accomplished first baseman. In 1967, at the age of 36, he handled more chances than any other first baseman in the major leagues and no regular first baseman anywhere committed fewer errors than he did.

That was the first renaissance of Ernie Banks. The second has been a running battle. For when Leo Durocher took over the Cubs as manager, he made it clear he was looking for somebody to succeed Ernie at first base. He kept bringing up prospects from the minor leagues and importing prospects from other teams. None of them could make it; Ernie always reclaimed his position at first base. "I've 'retired' him three years in a row," said Leo Durocher candidly—and admiringly—late last season, "but he doesn't stay 'retired.' I guess he just gets tired of seeing these young kids I keep trying to put in his place."

One of the reasons that Banks still does so well is that he continuously studies his performance. The Cubs take pictures of every Chicago batter in every ball game. So when he was not altogether satisfied with his performance about one-third of the way through the 1968 season, he sat down to study films of himself. He found he had opened up his stance—"When you open up too soon, it means you're not following the ball." He also had been swinging poorly—"I had been winding up before I swung at the ball. That's not my natural way. Usually I move straight into the ball without winding up." He had also changed his bat: now he'd moved back to a heavier bat—one weighing 36 ounces. The reasons were simple: no longer was he swinging any bat with the eye-blinking speed of the past. So in order to keep the impact-at-contact up, he compensated for reduced speed by increasing mass—or weight—in the bat. In addition, he was trying to hit the ball to all fields—including right field—and the added "wood" on the bat made that prospect a little more successful. When he put it all together, he went out and worked on it in batting practice. "I'd keep telling myself, 'Move forward! Move forward, move forward!' " The idea was not to open up and move his stance and move in the direction of the pitcher but to move right into the ball. The first time he tried it in a game, he moved straight into a screwball thrown by Mike McCormick of the San Francisco Giants—and stroked it smoothly into the left-field bleachers. He went on to get 32 homers and set a number of Cub records—some of which went back to the 1880's and 1890's—for total bases and games played and at-bats—as well as continuing to break his own team records for home runs and extra-base hits.

There are two other reasons why Banks—at a somewhat tree-ripened age—has continued to prosper in the big leagues. One is that he maintains a superb physical condition. In the winter Banks launches a determined program at the local YMCA, doing calisthenics and playing handball—the latter for speed and reflexes. Then he goes out to Arizona before spring training opens and continues his conditioning process there—running and hiking, playing golf and handball, building up his endurance. From time to time, he and Billy Williams drive to Casa Grande, where the Giants work out, to take a dip in the warm baths of the area. The result: he played at a lower weight in 1968 than he had some five or ten years earlier.

The other reason is that Banks maintains an inner serenity. "Here is a man who never complains," said one of his teammates a few years ago. Not even during the torment of the move to first base—or the attempts to move him from first base onto the bench. For his part, the serene man at first base, Ernie Banks, merely expresses hope that he'll have a chance to do it again. And again. And again.

He will. For when the 1969 baseball season rises to its peak, and the sun is high and warm over Wrigley Field, the fortunes of the Cubs will rest again with Ernie Banks and Billy Williams—each in their way so different, each in their results so superbly the same.

BILL FURLONG is a prolific contributor to national magazine including Sport *and* Sports Illustrated. *He can be called on to comment, with perception, about almost anything—from curve balls to Chicago cops.*

ERNIE BANKS

Year	Club	Lea	Pos	AB	R	H	HR	RBI	Avg
1953	Chicago	N. L.	SS	35	3	11	2	6	.314
1954	Chicago	N. L.	SS	593	70	163	19	79	.275
1955	Chicago	N. L.	SS	596	98	176	44	117	.295
1956	Chicago	N. L.	SS	538	82	160	28	85	.297
1957	Chicago	N. L.	SS-3B	594	113	169	43	102	.285
1958	Chicago	N. L.	SS	617	119	193	47	129	.313
1959	Chicago	N. L.	SS	589	97	179	45	143	.304
1960	Chicago	N. L.	SS	597	94	162	41	117	.271
1961	Chicago	N. L.	SS-1B	511	75	152	29	80	.278
1962	Chicago	N. L.	1B-3B	610	87	164	37	104	.269
1963	Chicago	N. L.	1B	432	41	98	18	64	.227
1964	Chicago	N. L.	1B	591	67	156	23	95	.264
1965	Chicago	N. L.	1B	612	79	162	28	106	.265
1966	Chicago	N. L.	1B-3B	511	52	139	15	75	.272
1967	Chicago	N. L.	1B	573	68	158	23	95	.276
1968	Chicago	N. L.	1B	552	71	136	32	83	.246

BILLY WILLIAMS

Year	Club	Lea	Pos	AB	R	H	HR	RBI	Avg
1956	Ponca City	Soon. St.	OF	17	4	4	0	4	.235
1957	Ponca City	Soon. St.	OF	451	87	140	17	95	.310
1958	Pueblo	Western	OF	80	9	20	2	11	.250
1958	Burlington	Three-I	OF	214	38	65	10	38	.304
1959	San Antonio	Texas	1B-OF	371	57	118	10	79	.318
1959	Ft. Worth	A. A.	OF	21	7	10	1	5	.476
1959	Chicago	N. L.	OF	33	0	5	0	2	.152
1960	Houston	A. A.	OF	473	75	153	26	80	.323
1960	Chicago	N. L.	OF	47	4	13	2	7	.277
1961	Chicago	N. L.	OF	529	75	147	25	86	.278
1962	Chicago	N. L.	OF	618	94	184	22	92	.298
1963	Chicago	N. L.	OF	612	87	175	25	95	.286
1964	Chicago	N. L.	OF	645	100	201	33	98	.312
1965	Chicago	N. L.	OF	645	115	203	34	108	.315
1966	Chicago	N. L.	OF	648	100	179	29	91	.276
1967	Chicago	N. L.	OF	634	92	176	28	84	.278
1968	Chicago	N. L.	OF	642	91	185	30	98	.288

KEN HARRELSON

The Hawk Flies High

by RAY ROBINSON

Late in 1968, on the next to last day of the long baseball season, over 25,000 people journeyed to Fenway Park to see the Boston Red Sox battle for third-place money. This, to say the least, was a tribute to the enthusiasm and durability of Boston fandom.

But over the last two years a great metamorphosis has taken place in Boston baseball. First, in 1967, in the Year of the Yaz, the Red Sox clawed and rallied to an American League flag, then went to the seventh game in the World Series against the Cardinals, before Jim Lonborg's arm simply wore out.

Then, in '68, with Lonborg a victim of a fatuous skiing accident and Carl Yastrzemski felled, for the most part, by one-too-many off-season banquets, a new and entirely unexpected star rose on the Beantown horizon. His name was Kenneth Smith Harrelson, a man primarily known for his skills at pool and golf, the rakish cut of his blue blazer and his white turtleneck and his drawerful of monogrammed, multi-colored shirts.

The Hawk, which is what his admirers and friends have long called him, had a .236 lifetime batting average before 1968 got under way. His highest home-run figure before '68 had been 23 that he'd hit for Kansas City in 1965. In addition, his dubious skill at first base and the outfield had long placed him in the Ike Boone and Smead Jolley class.

Yet, this was the same Harrelson who, on the afternoon of September 29, 1968, was ejected from the Red Sox-Yankee game for arguing about a called third strike.

Then, instead of going home, he stuck around Fenway Park. And what did he do on this hardly eventful day? He engaged in some late-afternoon batting practice with a reserve catcher, Russ Nixon. Nixon pitched to the 6′ 2″, 195-pound slugger, while two coaches ran down his longitudinal drives in the gloom of the fall evening.

The difference between third place and fourth place would be about $800 a man. Ken Harrelson wanted that difference for himself and for his teammates. That the Red Sox didn't finish third was not his fault. He had given it his all—right to the bitter end. Generally considered a swinger, an eccentric and, as *Sports Illustrated* has reported, "a player drawn from the minds of Ring Lardner and Tom Wolfe," The Hawk surprised an awful lot of folks in Boston and elsewhere last year.

There's little doubt, for instance, that without Ken Harrelson the Red Sox would have occupied a disaster area in 1968. Harrelson's big bat rang out almost monotonously throughout the campaign. His 109 runs batted in not only led *all* American League hitters, including Frank Howard, who had 106, but also surpassed *all* National League sluggers. In 1965, with KC, Ken had knocked in 66 runs, hardly enough to qualify him for future stardom. But here he was, in 1968, showing the way to Yastrzemski, the Super-Star of all baseball in 1967.

During 1968 spring training in Florida, it did not appear likely that the Red Sox would retain Harrelson, who had come to them in 1967, after Charlie Finley, the voluble owner of the KC Athletics, had given The Hawk his "unconditional release." The Hawk, who was charged by Finley with having dubbed him a menace to baseball— or something equally as earth-shaking—then proceeded to put himself up to the highest bidder, an opportunity few ballplayers have had in recent years. Seven teams reportedly were interested in Harrelson's services, including some National League entries. But when Mr. Yawkey of Boston put together a small bundle worth about $75,000, plus a three-year contract, Harrelson decided he wanted to be taken along for the ride, as the Sox battled for a flag.

"I was making more money than I could count," said The Hawk, who had become the logical candidate to succeed the injured Tony Conigliaro in the minds and hearts of Boston fans. However, that was just so much theory. Ken batted .200 for the Red Sox in less than 25 games—which was not even as good as his performance in KC and Washington earlier in the season. When the Sox wound up in the Series he got into four games, played right field like he was catatonic, managed to buy one hit for an average of .077 and, in general, set himself up for another change of venue.

"I figured for sure that the Red Sox were going to trade me to Detroit or New York, where they needed right-handed power hitting," said Ken.

There he was, still talking up a storm about being a power-hitter, when the record fairly screeched that he was lucky to be in the majors.

But the realities of life soon confronted the Red Sox: they simply couldn't dispense with this oddball because Conigliaro's eyesight was still troubling him and first baseman George Scott was having difficulty hitting his weight (215).

So The Hawk remained in Boston, with his flashy mod wardrobe, his perennial sunglasses and his close-to-shoulder-length hair that might give some paranoids apoplexy. "I'm glad we didn't get any good offers for him," says Manager Dick Williams. "We wouldn't be where we are without him—and I probably wouldn't be here now, either."

As the 1968 season wore on, it became obvious that the Red Sox weren't going to repeat their "impossible dream" year of 1967. But it also became obvious that The Hawk, whose sartorial habits have put Lippy Leo Durocher into the ranks of the squares and the conservatives, had emerged not only as the year's most unexpected star—but as Boston's most popular citizen, after Yaz.

"He's done everything I haven't been able to do," acknowledged Yaz, the triple crown dynamo of 1967.

Others on the Red Sox, including shortstop Rico Petrocelli, thought Harrelson was all that separated the team from last place. "That's where we'd be without him," said Rico.

In the first half of the season Harrelson, freed from the restraints of managers who failed to appreciate his lifestyle (at Washington, where Ken toiled briefly under Gil Hodges, the latter, generally a tolerant man, failed to understand why a ballplayer, even if he felt like Samson, had to look like him), bombed out enough hits to win a dozen games by himself. Most of the time The Hawk was there with a clutch home run when the Sox needed it. During one spell, Harrelson played in 64 games and knocked in 60 runs.

So effective was Harrelson's hitting performance that American League managers started to set up a special defense against him. The last time they had done that to thwart a Bostonian, they called it the Williams Shift. Now they called it the Harrelson Shift, where the second baseman was stationed on the left side of the base. In this arrangement, the first baseman becomes responsible for the entire right side of the infield. Harrelson rewarded such consideration by occasionally poking one to the opposite field (he is a righty batter) or, like his predecessor, trying to cram one down the throats of the neatly aligned foe.

In those thrilling down-to-the-wire days of the '67 flag chase, "Yaz, Sir, That's My Baby" buttons helped to garnish the New England landscape. Last year, while Harrelson worked on his extensive wardrobe, which one couturier suggests embraces 40 sports jackets, two green Nehru suits and 100 pairs of slacks and simultaneously built his batting average to .275, the adoring fans in Fenway's right-field bleachers substituted their "Hawk-It-To-'Em-Sox" banners for their Yaz buttons. It was apparent that the rebel from Woodruff, South Carolina (his birthplace), and Savannah, Georgia (where his family moved), had made it big with the New England Irish and the Yankee constituency.

The extent of the love affair with this man, who is to baseball what long side-burned Joe Namath is to pro football and what Muhammad Ali once was to boxing, became increasingly clear by the end of the season.

As the Yanks played at Fenway Park on the last Friday night of the year, Harrelson banged out two hits. But even more interesting was the relative reaction to the other celebrities on hand, including Mickey Mantle, the fragile but courageous *grise eminence* of the Yanks, Elston Howard, the veteran Boston catcher playing his final year, and Yaz.

When Mantle batted the first time, over 28,000 fans gave him a rousing standing ovation. Last year almost every time Mickey came to bat fans treated him like a king making a final appearance before his subjects. Mantle, like Jack Dempsey, has become more popular, as his talents have lessened.

When Yaz hit a two-run homer, the natives gave him a sitting ovation—and when Howard pinch-hit for the Red Sox in the eighth inning, he earned a "semi-standing ovation," in the words of reporter George Vecsey of the New York *Times.*

But with The Hawk, it was different: a delegation of boys and girls journeyed out to visit him in right field, where he stood in all of his beefy glory, both of his wrists taped in a baseball version of slave bracelets. Three young girls were among those who made the fateful pilgrimage.

When Manager Williams removed Harrelson late in the game, it was suggested he did so to save Ken from bodily harm. Others insisted the move was designed to save the grass for the impending football season.

Today Ken Harrelson, an old married man of 26 (he was in his late teens when he deserted the world's fun-loving bachelors), is ten years away from the original $30,000 bonus he got for signing with the Kansas City A's. But he is light years away from those years of indecisiveness and immaturity.

"Some guys," he says, "grow up when they're 18 or 19. It took me until I was 25."

He is the hook-nosed man who delights in being called The Super-Hawk (without the war connotation, of course) and he is tickled with his spiked shoes and his shirts that are inscribed with that single most dramatic word of all, "HAWK."

And what tickles him most of all is that the staid citizenry of Boston doesn't care what he wears as long as he keeps swinging, both on and off field.

"Just so long as he keeps banging that ball," says Dick Williams, "he can show up in his athletic supporter."

The Hawk, who could, in his own eyes, have been the world's top golfer or basketball player, or maybe even the best arm wrestler, feels that's real good thinking. It helps him love everybody, even those who prefer crew cuts.

KEN HARRELSON

Year	Club	Lea	Pos	AB	R	H	HR	RBI	Avg
1959	Olean	N.Y.-Pa.	OF	120	9	23	2	8	.192
1960	Sanford	Fla.-St.	1B-3B	472	70	107	10	72	.227
1961	Visalia	Calif.	1B-3B-OF	535	94	161	25	114	.301
1962	Binghampton	Eastern	1B-OF	536	89	146	38	138	.272
1963	Portland	P. C.	OF-1B	160	27	48	9	31	.300
1963	Kansas City	A. L.	1B-OF	226	16	52	6	23	.230
1964	Dallas	P. C.	OF-1B	271	53	63	18	52	.232
1964	Kansas City	A. L.	OF-1B	139	15	27	7	12	.194
1965	Kansas City	A. L.	1B-OF	483	61	115	23	66	.238
1966	K. C.-Wash.	A. L.	1B-OF	460	49	109	12	50	.237
1967	Wash.-K. C.-Boston	A. L.	1B-OF	333	42	85	12	54	.255
1968	Boston	A. L.	1B-OF	535	79	147	35	109	.275
World Series									
1967	Boston	A. L.	OF	13	0	1	0	1	.077

APPENDIX A—FINAL STANDINGS 1968

NATIONAL LEAGUE

	W	L	Pc	GB
St. Louis	97	65	.599	—
San Francisco	88	74	.543	9
Chicago	84	78	.519	13
Cincinnati	83	79	.512	14
Atlanta	81	81	.500	16
Pittsburgh	80	82	.494	17
Los Angeles	76	86	.469	21
Philadelphia	76	86	.469	21
New York	73	89	.451	24
Houston	72	90	.444	25

AMERICAN LEAGUE

	W	L	Pc	GB
Detroit	103	59	.636	—
Baltimore	91	71	.562	12
Cleveland	86	75	.534	16½
Boston	86	76	.531	17
New York	83	79	.512	20
Oakland	82	80	.506	21
Minnesota	79	83	.488	24
California	67	95	.414	36
Chicago	67	95	.414	36
Washington	65	96	.404	37½

APPENDIX B—WORLD SERIES 1968

FIRST GAME

											R.	H.	E.
Tigers	0	0	0		0	0	0		0	0	0—0	5	3
Cardinals	0	0	0		3	0	0		1	0	x—4	6	0

Batteries—McLain, Dobson (6), McMahon (8) and Freehan; Gibson and McCarver.
Losing pitcher—McLain.
Home run—St. Louis: Brock.
Attendance: 54,692.

SECOND GAME

Tigers	0	1	1		0	0	3		1	0	2—8	13	1
Cardinals	0	0	0		0	0	1		0	0	0—1	6	0

Batteries—Lolich and Freehan; Briles, Carlton (6), Willis (7), Hoerner (9) and McCarver.
Losing pitcher—Briles.
Home runs—Detroit: Horton, Lolich, Cash.
Attendance: 54,692.

THIRD GAME

Cardinals	0	0	0		0	4	0		3	0	0—7	13	0
Tigers	0	0	2		0	1	0		0	0	0—3	4	0

Batteries—Washburn, Hoerner (6) and McCarver; Wilson, Dobson (5), McMahon (6), Patterson (7), Hiller (8) and Freehan.
Winning pitcher—Washburn. Losing pitcher—Wilson.
Home runs—St. Louis: McCarver, Cepeda. Detroit: Kaline, McAuliffe.
Attendance: 53,634.

FOURTH GAME

Cardinals	2	0	2		2	0	0		0	4	0—10	13	0
Tigers	0	0	0		1	0	0		0	0	0—1	5	4

Batteries—Gibson and McCarver; McLain, Sparma (3), Patterson (4), Lasher (6), Hiller (8), Dobson (8) and Freehan.
Winning pitcher—Gibson. Losing pitcher—McLain.
Home runs—St. Louis: Brock, Gibson. Detroit: Northrup.
Attendance: 53,634.

FIFTH GAME

Cardinals	3	0	0		0	0	0		0	0	0—3	9	0
Tigers	0	0	0		2	0	0		3	0	x—5	9	1

Batteries—Briles, Hoerner (7), Willis (7) and McCarver; Lolich and Freehan.
Winning pitcher—Lolich. Losing pitcher—Hoerner.
Home run—St. Louis: Cepeda.
Attendance: 53,634.

SIXTH GAME

Tigers	0	2	10		0	1	0		0	0	0—13	12	1
Cardinals	0	0	0		0	0	0		0	0	1—1	9	1

Batteries—McLain and Freehan; Washburn, Jaster (3), Willis (3), Hughes (3), Carlton (4), Granger (7), Nelson (9) and McCarver.
Losing pitcher—Washburn.
Home runs—Detroit: Northrup, Kaline.
Attendance: 54,692.

SEVENTH GAME

Tigers	0	0	0		0	0	0		3	0	1—4	8	1
Cardinals	0	0	0		0	0	0		0	0	1—1	5	0

Batteries—Lolich and Freehan; Gibson and McCarver.
Home run—St. Louis: Shannon.
Attendance: 54,692.

WORLD SERIES TOTALS—1968

DETROIT TIGERS

	G	AB	R	H	2B	3B	HR	RBI	BB	SO	Bat. Avg.	PO	A	E	Avg. Fldg.
McAuliffe, 2b	7	27	5	6	0	0	1	3	4	6	.222	11	16	0	1.000
Stanley, ss	7	28	4	6	0	1	0	0	2	4	.214	15	16	2	.939
Kaline, rf	7	29	6	11	2	0	2	8	0	7	.379	18	0	0	1.000
Cash, 1b	7	26	5	10	0	0	1	5	3	5	.385	59	6	2	.970
Horton, lf	7	23	6	7	1	1	1	3	5	6	.304	5	1	1	.857
Northrup, cf	7	28	4	7	0	1	2	8	1	5	.250	22	0	2	.917
Freehan, c	7	24	0	2	1	0	0	2	4	8	.083	45	6	2	.962
Wert, 3b	6	17	1	2	0	0	0	2	6	5	.118	5	14	0	1.000
Mathews	2	3	0	1	0	0	0	0	1	1	.333	0	1	1	.500
Tracewski, 3b	2	0	1	0	0	0	0	0	0	0	.000	0	0	0	.000
McLain, p	3	6	0	0	0	0	0	0	0	4	.000	0	3	1	.750
Matchick	3	3	0	0	0	0	0	0	0	1	.000	0	0	0	.000
Dobson, p	3	3	0	0	0	0	0	0	0	0	.000	-1	0	0	1.000
Brown	1	1	0	0	0	0	0	0	0	0	.000	0	0	0	.000
McMahon, p	2	0	0	0	0	0	0	0	0	0	.000	1	0	0	1.000
Lolich, p	3	12	2	3	0	0	1	2	1	5	.250	1	4	0	1.000
Oyler, ss	4	0	0	0	0	0	0	0	0	0	.000	2	0	0	1.000
Wilson, p	1	1	0	0	0	0	0	0	0	1	.000	0	2	0	1.000
Patterson, p	2	0	0	0	0	0	0	0	0	0	.000	1	0	0	1.000
Comer	1	1	0	1	0	0	0	0	0	0	1.000	0	0	0	.000
Hiller, p	2	0	0	0	0	0	0	0	0	0	.000	1	0	0	1.000
Price	2	2	0	0	0	0	0	0	0	1	.000	0	0	0	.000
Sparma, p	1	0	0	0	0	0	0	0	0	0	.000	0	0	0	.000
Lasher, p	1	0	0	0	0	0	0	0	0	0	.000	0	1	0	1.000
Total	7	231	34	56	4	3	8	33	27	59	.242	186	71	11	.959

ST. LOUIS CARDINALS

	G	AB	R	H	2B	3B	HR	RBI	BB	SO	Bat. Avg.	PO	A	E	Avg. Fldg.
Brock, lf	7	28	6	13	3	1	2	5	3	4	.464	13	0	1	.929
Flood, cf	7	28	4	8	1	0	0	2	2	2	.286	13	0	0	1.000
Maris, rf	6	19	5	3	1	0	0	1	3	3	.158	8	0	0	1.000
Cepeda, 1b	7	28	2	7	0	0	2	6	2	3	.250	48	4	0	1.000
McCarver, c	7	27	3	9	0	2	1	4	3	2	.333	61	1	0	1.000
Shannon, 3b	7	29	3	8	1	0	1	4	1	5	.276	5	10	1	.938
Javier, 2b	7	27	1	9	1	0	0	3	3	4	.333	14	14	0	1.000
Maxvill, ss	7	22	1	0	0	0	0	0	3	5	.000	15	14	0	1.000
Gibson, p	3	8	2	1	0	0	1	2	1	2	.125	2	0	0	1.000
Davis, rf	2	7	0	0	0	0	0	0	0	2	.000	5	0	0	1.000
Briles, p	2	4	0	0	0	0	0	0	0	4	.000	0	2	0	1.000
Carlton, p	2	0	0	0	0	0	0	0	0	0	.000	1	1	0	1.000
Willis, p	3	0	0	0	0	0	0	0	0	0	.000	1	0	0	1.000
Gagliano	3	3	0	0	0	0	0	0	0	0	.000	0	0	0	.000
Hoerner, p	3	2	0	1	0	0	0	0	0	1	.500	0	0	0	.000
Washburn, p	2	3	0	0	0	0	0	0	0	1	.000	0	1	0	1.000
Spiezio	1	1	0	1	0	0	0	0	0	0	1.000	0	0	0	.000
Schofield	2	0	0	0	0	0	0	0	0	0	.000	0	0	0	.000
Jaster, p	1	0	0	0	0	0	0	0	0	0	.000	0	0	0	.000
Hughes, p	1	0	0	0	0	0	0	0	0	0	.000	0	0	0	.000
Ricketts	1	1	0	1	0	0	0	0	0	0	1.000	0	0	0	.000
Granger, p	1	0	0	0	0	0	0	0	0	0	.000	0	1	0	1.000
Tolan	1	1	0	0	0	0	0	0	0	1	.000	0	0	0	.000
Edwards	1	1	0	0	0	0	0	0	0	1	.000	0	0	0	.000
Nelson, p	1	0	0	0	0	0	0	0	0	0	.000	0	0	0	.000
Total	7	239	27	61	7	3	7	27	21	40	.255	186	48	2	.991

PITCHING RECORDS

Detroit Tigers

	G	CG	IP	H	R	BB	SO	HB	WP	W	L	ER	ERA
McLain	3	1	16⅔	18	8	4	13	0	0	1	2	6	3.18
Dobson	3	0	4⅔	5	2	1	0	0	0	0	0	2	3.60
McMahon	2	0	2	4	3	0	1	0	0	0	0	3	18.00
Lolich	3	3	27	20	5	6	21	1	0	3	0	5	1.67
Wilson	1	0	4⅓	4	3	6	3	0	0	0	1	3	6.75
Patterson	2	0	3	1	0	1	0	0	0	0	0	0	0.00
Hiller	2	0	2	6	4	3	1	0	0	0	0	3	18.00
Lasher	1	0	2	1	0	0	1	0	0	0	0	0	0.00
Sparma	1	0	⅓	2	2	0	0	0	0	0	0	2	54.00
Total	7	4	62	61	27	21	40	1	0	4	3	24	3.48

St. Louis Cardinals

	G	CG	IP	H	R	BB	SO	HB	WP	W	L	ER	ERA
Gibson	3	3	27	18	5	4	35	0	0	2	1	5	1.67
Briles	2	0	11⅓	13	7	4	7	0	0	0	1	7	5.73
Carlton	2	0	4	7	3	1	3	0	0	0	0	3	6.75
Willis	3	0	4⅓	2	4	4	3	1	0	0	0	4	9.00
Hoerner	3	0	4⅔	5	4	5	3	0	0	0	1	2	3.85
Washburn	2	0	7⅓	7	8	7	6	0	0	1	1	8	9.82
Jaster	1	0	2	2	3	1	0	0	0	0	0	3	
Hughes	1	0	⅓	2	0	0	0	0	0	0	0	0	0.00
Granger	1	0	2	0	0	1	1	2	0	0	0	0	0.00
Nelson	1	0	1	0	0	0	1	0	0	0	0	0	0.00
Total	7	3	62	56	34	27	59	3	0	3	4	32	4.65

COMPOSITE SCORE BY INNINGS

Detroit	0	3	13	3	2	3	7	0	3—34
St. Louis	5	0	2	5	4	1	4	4	2—27

Stolen Bases—Brock 7, Javier, Flood 3. Sacrifices—Gibson, Oyler, McLain. Sacrifice Fly—Cash. Double Plays—Stanley, McAuliffe and Cash; Maxvill and Cepeda; Freehan and Wert; Javier, Maxvill and Cepeda; Cepeda, Maxvill; Shannon, Javier and Cepeda; Stanley, McAuliffe and Cash; Maxvill, Javier and Cepeda; Granger, Maxvill and Cepeda; Stanley and Cash. Left on Bases—Detroit 44, St. Louis 49.

Umpires—Honochick (A.), Landis, (N.), Kinnamon (A.), Harvey (N.), Haller (A.), Gorman (N.).

Time of Games—2:29 (first game); 2:41 (second game); 3:17 (third game); 2:34 (fourth game); 2:43 (fifth game); 2:26 (sixth game); 2:07 (seventh game).